POWER MOVES

The Life and Legacy of a
Black Chamber Executive

By John E. Harmon Sr. IOM

This work reflects actual events in the life of the author as truthfully as recollection permits. Some events have been compressed, and some dialogue has been recreated.

Copyright 2025 by John E. Harmon Sr.

For more information, address:

jharmon@aaccnj.com
Paperback ISBN: 979-8-9921744-1-0
eBook ISBN: 979-8-9921744-2-7
Hardcover ISBN: 979-8-9921744-0-3
www.aaccnj.com

Dedication

This book is dedicated to my three sons, John Jr., Joshua, and Justin, and to the memory of their mother, Lennice, who departed this world much too soon. Each phrase, course of action, life changing decision and strategic engagement mentioned in this book was intended to bring forth a purposeful life for myself, while realizing the dreams of many and toward a favorable impact within society.

From the inception of my journey, there were a multitude of investors, some whose contributions were more equitable than others, but all of which were essential. In the end, it taught me that it does not have to be your vision for you to own it or reshape it. When you lead with heart, the execution will always lead to a meaningful impact and with results that go on to form your legacy— a life that leaves those around you inspired and overwhelmingly proud.

Table Of Contents

Introduction

The Courage To Fail

I remember the moment vividly; a blend of relief and sadness washed over me as I scribbled my name down on the signature line. After eight years of living in our dream home, my wife and I made the difficult but necessary decision to deed the property back to the bank. I was relieved that the lender had agreed to the deal, and that I'd found us another home to live in – something significantly smaller and much more modest. Still, I was disappointed that I'd veered my family to such a somber phase in our lives.

I stared down at the deed for our new home, the ink still wet from where I'd just signed, and felt a sinking feeling in the pit of my stomach. There are very few things in this world that can injure a man's spirit as deeply as the feeling of letting his own family down. Needless to say, I felt like a failure.

It was 1995, and we had just moved into the new house. As I led my wife and three young sons to the front door, which, admittedly, was in desperate need of some TLC, I could see the confused looks on their faces. Before even stepping foot inside, it was clear that it was a downgrade from our previous home.

It was much smaller, and the paint on the exterior was faded and peeling throughout. Inside, the rooms were tiny and cramped, and paled in comparison to the fine dwellings my boys had grown accustomed to. There was no central air. The ceiling on the second floor was so low, I had to stoop down for fear of my head grazing the wall above me.

I watched as my kids' eyes inspected every corner, wondering how it would fit all of our stuff. I knew they missed our old home, the one where they'd spent nearly their entire lives. I missed it too. This wasn't how it was supposed to be. Inside, I felt like we were moving backwards but I did my best to keep everyone's spirits high.

For now, at least, this new place was the best we could do. As an entrepreneur, I was required to make sacrifices to keep the business afloat. And as a husband and father, I had to provide for my family, to ensure they were safe and secure, and that all of their needs were met. Unfortunately, those two realities don't always exist in harmony, and I was learning that lesson the hard way.

The trucking company I'd started with my brother, Eddie, was struggling, with money leaking out faster than it flowed in. And as hard as we worked to try to get us out of the choppy, precarious waters we were sailing in, it never seemed to be enough.

I started the company, Harmon Transfer Corp., in 1989, after leaving my job in banking. At first, we had just one truck, purchased using my severance pay, and one driver: Eddie. My father had convinced me to get a driver's license to share in the driving, as I had no business running a company if I couldn't do the work myself. So, I did. And eventually, we expanded to two trucks. After six months, we were able to hire several drivers, increasing our truck count to four. It was no easy road, but we were steadily growing. With a few lucrative contracts now under our belt, I was constantly thinking about ways to make the business even more profitable.

Unlike a lot of the other truck drivers I'd encountered, many of whom had very limited education, I was a college graduate. With a successful career in banking before entering the trucking industry, it helped me to see things a little differently from my colleagues. I had a keen eye for recognizing opportunities and I was intentional about the growth I wanted to see. Even before I started my company, I'd already thought long and hard about what it would take to *sustain* a business.

On Saturday mornings, I'd wake up early and head to a local diner where us truckers would gather to swap war stories. I was young in comparison to many of the others, and the OG's loved imparting their wisdom on me. I was happy to sop it all up and learn from these men, many of whom had spent the majority of their lives at the helm of a truck. They taught me things you'd never find in any textbook or manual, sharing lessons that could only be learned by years (sometimes decades) on the road.

To me, being an entrepreneur was the best way to provide for my family. I considered it to be a legacy I was leaving behind, for them to pick up and continue, if they so chose to. Unfortunately, my wife wasn't so enthusiastic about the whole thing. But I understood her reasoning. Entrepreneurship is risky. Sure, there's the possibility of bringing in a lot of cash and ceilingless profits. Plus you aren't bound to an employer who tells you what to do, when to do it or how to do it. But while there's a sense of freedom, of liberation from the constraints of traditional employment, there's also a dark and scary flipside to that coin: twenty-hour workdays with little to no days off; the crippling responsibility of having so many other people dependent on you and your success; the lack of stability, and the reality that the livelihood of your family is sometimes hanging on by a thread.

That precarious place was exactly where my family and I now found ourselves, hinging on the edge of losing everything. I'd made the decision to uproot and downsize our lives. My business wasn't failing by any means, but some of my equipment was. If I'd had better, more reliable trucks and trailers, we'd be in the perfect position to scale and grow the company. I needed an injection of cash to get us back to a healthy spot, and I knew that there were avenues out there for entrepreneurs to turn. I'd worked in banking before, so I knew the kinds of loans they gave out to business owners to help them fund and operate their projects.

With a business plan all figured out, I approached the New Jersey Economic Development Authority (NJEDA) – an organization that provides capital to businesses – with my proposal. I'd worked out that I needed $350,000 to purchase three refurbished trucks, three used trailers, and some cash for working capital. They told me that if I could get the Small Business Administration to issue a guarantee, they'd grant me the loan. Following their advice, I went to Carnegie Bank to apply for an SBA loan, and much to my relief, it was approved.

I felt the weight of my responsibilities instantly lift. The pressure I'd felt wearing down on me, over having to provide for my family and pay my staff, eased slightly. I was about to get the loan and we'd finally, *finally*, be out of the red. For the first time in months, I felt like I could breathe again. I went back to the NJEDA with the update, ready to collect the money they'd promised me. But instead of matching my enthusiasm, they reneged on their promise. They weren't going to give me the loan after all.

I was gutted. I'd spent so much time advocating for myself, creating a business plan, going back and forth between organizations, only to have them slam the door in my face. But with a laundry list of people depending on me, I didn't have time to sit around and feel sorry for myself. Beyond my employees, I still had a family to feed, and self-pity wasn't going to pay the bills or put food on the table.

It was 1997 and in the midst of my furious efforts to get my business back on track, I reconnected with someone I knew from my days working in banking. His name was William Granville, a Black executive with Mobil Oil Corporation executive that I'd met on the train while commuting to New York from Jersey. Bill told me that he, and 20 other business professionals, were getting ready to launch a Black Chamber of Commerce in Trenton.

Black businesses made up a big chunk of our city's economy, yet we lacked a collective to promote and protect our interests or to help connect us to sources of funding. I knew from my own experiences how difficult it had been to advocate for myself to gain access to the capital I needed. Through my background in banking, I was aware of what kinds of things they wanted to hear from loan applicants and knew how to best position myself for success. And yet, even with all that knowledge and know-how, I still wasn't able to secure the funds.

As soon as I heard about what the group was attempting to do, I had to be involved; it sounded like the answer to my prayers. I joined, becoming the group's 21st member. Together, we put $1,000 each into a pot to help fund the organization. We knew that to get the chamber going, and to have it become something that Black businesses could leverage to give our people a voice in the city's growing economy, it required that we all pitch in.

By then, most of the positions in the organization had already been taken. But there was still a role I could fill: chaplain. That's right, my career working in Black Chambers of Commerce was to sit back, listen, and lead the group in prayer. At the time, I was more than okay with that. It gave me the opportunity to learn more about what it took to run the organization from the inside. I didn't know anything about assembling a board of directors, creating bylaws, developing a system of governance, or sustaining a calendar of events, so I was content with observing and absorbing as much information as I could.

When I first got involved with the Metropolitan Trenton African American Chamber of Commerce, I still thought of myself as a trucking guy. My goals in life were still very much tethered to my business. I could barely imagine a future where I wasn't busy with transport contracts or when I didn't spend my Saturday mornings sipping hot tea in a diner parking lot with other truck drivers. Back then, I still believed that heading up Harmon Transfer Corp. was how I'd be an effective provider for my family. But after some time at the Chamber of Commerce, I began to realize that I was meant to have a bigger and more meaningful impact on the world.

I chose to begin my story with a moment of failure because that's what it took for me to truly find my purpose. The difficult moments I encountered prepared me for a life of advocacy for other Black business owners like myself. It forced me to journey through the struggles and tribulations of being a Black entrepreneur to gain clarity on how deeply we needed mechanisms of support.

It was at that time that I began to realize how interconnected my success was to the success of other Black folks. When I made it my goal to advocate for the collective advancement of Black folks in business, it improved not only the conditions within my own home, but the conditions of so many other Black business owners, too.

Chapter 1

Fish Bones and Chocolate Cake

Decades before I ever launched my own business, I dipped my toes into the pool of entrepreneurship for the very first time. Almost immediately, I was obsessed with the possibilities that it opened up to me; the potential that unfolded like a map, guiding me straight to freedom.

I was 11 years old. My dad's cousin, who I called Uncle Cliff, would drive up from Virginia with boxes full of sweet potatoes, tomatoes, cucumbers, watermelons, and cabbage, all stacked into his truck bed. I loved sitting back there, the colorful mosaic of produce surrounding me. I was tasked with helping Uncle Cliff sell the vegetables at the flea market in New Egypt, New Jersey. As he bartered with clients, I stuffed their orders into cardboard boxes and bags, and helped carry them to their cars.

Uncle Cliff didn't pay me very much, but I didn't need a lot. I was content with just having some extra money to line my pockets and freshen up my wardrobe. One of the first things I bought myself was a brand-new pair of Converse sneakers. They cost $6.95, which was a hell of a lot more money than the $3 Bobos my parents made me wear. One day, when there was a lull in customers, I walked around the flea market checking out the goods other people were selling. I spotted a lawnmower and instantly recognized it as more than a simple tool to mow the lawn – it was an opportunity for me to make even more money.

With the cash I made from Uncle Cliff, I bought the lawnmower and immediately returned home, going door to door offering to cut my neighbors' grass, for a small price, of course. From there, the ideas snowballed. Every season that came, I found another service I could offer; shovel snow, rake leaves or clear basements. There were so many small tedious jobs no one had the time to do. The possibilities were endless, and I was hooked.

*****

I grew up in a rowhouse in a working-class neighborhood of Trenton, New Jersey. The North Ward, as we called it, was home to many of the city's factory hands and other blue-collar workers. On most days, the neighborhood came alive before sunrise, with the streets busy with the rush of bodies hurrying to work.

Trenton was a mecca for various industries – ceramics, tile, iron, steel, rubber, paper, textiles, commercial freezers; we had it all. Many families had come here from the south, attracted to the promise of steady employment in the city's many industrial plants and factories, and the economic rewards that entailed. Our family was no different, though we were drawn in by a different resource – potatoes.

My parents, Adair and Vivian, met in Virginia, where they were both born. Mom was from a tiny town on the Eastern Shore called Wattsville, and she was the youngest of 24 children (of which only 18 survived). My dad, on the other hand, came from a family of farm contractors who specialized in potatoes.

Following the birth of my second oldest brother Kenny, my parents migrated north to Trenton for the potato season. My dad eventually established his own trucking business with his father, who we called Big Daddy. Big Daddy ran a potato processing plant in Robbinsville, about 10 miles from Trenton, called FH Valshing. There, they harvested the potatoes, packed them up and shipped them all over the country. My mother would work shifts at the plant sometimes too, sorting out the good potatoes from the bad ones as they moved down the conveyor belt, before bagging them up and stacking them on pallets where they'd be loaded up on the back of my father's trucks.

When she wasn't working at the plant, my mother worked at local electric companies doing piecework. Her job was to assemble different devices and extension cords, and at the end she'd get paid based on how many she'd completed.

My parents were the hardest working people I knew. After spending an entire day on her feet, sorting potatoes or coiling extension cords, my mom would come home and make dinner, ensure all of us kids had completed our homework, tidy up, and attend to any outstanding tasks that required her attention. There was very little in the house my mom couldn't or didn't do. In addition to managing the family's money and making sure the bills were paid on time, she also took care of the logistical side of the trucking business. If there was paperwork to be filled out, invoices to be mailed or workers to be paid, my mom was on top of it.

My dad tended to the hands-on side of the business. He was up every morning, hours before dawn, getting ready to hit the road. But his role went beyond driving the trucks and managing the shipments. He also handled the equipment, fixed any repairs, and supervised the workers. He had strong principles and a code of ethics that were set in gold. And he expected all of us to abide by them.

He showed us, me and my brothers, how to patch a flat tire on the tractors and trailers. He taught us to remove the lug nuts and to break the tire off the rim, to fix the leaks, and then put everything back together again. It was a tedious, grueling process, and we were expected to do it no matter how cold or wet it was outside. If he came home from work and told us "I got one," or "I got two," we knew that we had to get out there and fix the flats before he left for work again the next morning.

The same went for our household chores. We were all assigned a job to do for the week, whether that was washing dishes, cleaning the yard or mopping the floor. And if your chores weren't completed, there'd be hell to pay.

One morning, at around 3 a.m., Dad strode into the kitchen to get himself something to eat before work. He noticed a stack of plates and pots sitting in the sink, unwashed, and all hell broke loose. He woke all of us kids up, demanding to know how we could go to sleep with dirty dishes in the sink. This inevitably led to a huge fight, with all of us yelling at each other over whose job it had been, and who should have to do them. In the end, it didn't really matter. None of us could go back to bed until the dishes were cleared.

Truthfully, this was considered a mild punishment. Dad was the disciplinarian in the house and had his own personal brand of reprimanding us. It usually involved a belt and a painful thrashing. This created a confusing dichotomy for me, one I sometimes struggled to come to terms with. On the one hand, he was unquestionably my hero. Sure, he hadn't finished high school, and he could barely read or write, but he moved through the world with a quiet, self-assured confidence that made his shortcomings seem insignificant. It didn't matter if he struggled to read a map, because he didn't need it anyway. With his mind being the only navigation tool he needed, he always figured out the way there. He was also a self-taught mechanic who learned how to repair the trucks and trailers on his own. Regardless of what the weather was like outside – rain, sleet or snow – Dad was out there, pecking away at the problem until it was fixed. His work ethic was inspiring, and I grew up wanting to be just like him, to emulate his mannerisms, way of speaking, and the principled way he carried himself. I even developed an enduring passion for trucking, something that was no doubt motivated by his influence.

But on the other hand, Dad had a wicked and vicious temper. As a kid, it was hard to reconcile that your hero was also the one beating you up. It took very little provocation to move him to violence, and if we got into his sights, he would pummel us without mercy. I found myself more mad than sad in those moments, my feelings of vulnerability morphing into anger at the perceived injustice. I was defenseless against him; it wasn't like I could hit him back, nor did I want to. He loved to lob the 'golden rule' at us, to remind us to treat others how we wanted to be treated. But he didn't seem so keen on taking his own advice when he took his anger out on us, or Mom.

As I got older, I recognized that I didn't have to like everything about him. It's like when you get a good piece of fish. You eat the flesh and try your best to avoid the bones. That's how it was with Dad. I kept the good parts, which were overwhelming and fulfilling, and I threw away the negative aspects. I knew that he loved us, me and my siblings, and I definitely knew that he loved Mom. But I had to learn at a young age that he showed it in his own way. He was never really one to express his feelings, at least not with words. To him, love was waking up every morning, no matter how sick or tired he was feeling, and dragging himself to work. It was spending six days a week in the cabin of a semi-truck, rarely ever sleeping through a full night. To Dad, love was action. I don't think he thought it was necessary to make us *feel* loved by him when his sacrifices proved his point even more saliently.

My mother always made up for my dad's limitations when it came to offering affection. I was the sixth of seven children, and the youngest of five boys. As you can imagine, I spent a lot of time running after my older brothers, begging them to play with me. And they spent equally as much time running away from me.

When they headed outside to play ball, I'd chase behind them, my little legs moving as fast as they could. "Wait up!" I'd shout, convincing myself they'd simply forgotten to invite me. By the time I made it to the gate, they'd already slammed it shut and were halfway down the street, far out of my reach. I'd stand there for a moment, completely still, willing them to come back. When I didn't hear their footsteps stomping back toward the closed gate, my eyes would fill with tears and I'd shuffle back to the house, crying.

Call it a mother's intuition, if you will, but Mom would always be waiting there at the door for me with her arms wide open. To distract me from my pain, she'd take me to the kitchen and lay out a bunch of ingredients on the counter; flour, sugar, milk, eggs, butter, and cocoa. I'd watch as she strategically mixed all the components together in carefully measured amounts, before popping the concoction into the oven. Soon enough, the sweet smell of chocolate cake would waft through the house, and I'd sit by the oven, eagerly waiting for it to be done. That's how my mom was. She had a way of making you forget you were sad or upset.

Growing up in our house could be confusing sometimes, caught in the tug-of-war between Mom's gentle spirit and Dad's violent streak. But for the most part, my siblings and I got along well, allowing our home to be a peaceful and lively place.

As one of seven kids, it was difficult to establish my own identity amongst my siblings, to find out where I fit and who I was. My brothers Eddie, Kenny, Nate, and Dwight all played baseball, so naturally, I was expected to share that same passion for the game.

When I was nine, my mom signed me up for the local Little League team. At first, I was excited. I'd watched my brothers play in the lot behind our house, beaming with pride whenever they'd hit a home run. Wanting so badly to follow in their footsteps, I was intent on proving myself. But as I lined up in the batter's box for the first time, something unexpected happened. I went up to bat and as the first pitch came flying towards me, I flinched in terror and instinctively jumped back. I tried my best to shake off the fear, to give it another go. But again, as the pitcher loaded up and tossed the ball in my direction, my body leapt backwards. It turns out, the game just didn't appeal to me in the same way it had for my brothers. Still, I convinced myself that there were other ways to establish myself, I just hadn't found them yet.

Outside of my siblings, I'd acquired my own group of friends; boys I hung out with from the neighborhood. My best friend was a boy named Corkie, who lived down the block. Along with Shane, Suge, Hobbs, and Moland, we spent everyday together after school, riding our bikes or playing kick soccer.

Behind the rowhouses where we lived, there was a large vacant lot that had once been a salvage yard owned by a body shop nearby. After they'd removed all of the cars, us neighborhood kids got together and cleaned the space up. We raked the broken glass into piles and cleared away the trash, revealing a wide-open expanse. We erected a basketball court and set up bases for a baseball diamond. While Corkie, Moland, Hobbs and I tossed around a football, the girls, including my sisters Paulette and Arlene, skipped rope and chased us. My parents would let us stay out there all day, playing and doing what kids did. But they had one rule that we couldn't disobey: as soon as the streetlights came on, you got your butt home. And we listened, unwilling to find out what would happen if we didn't.

And it was probably for the best that we listened. Our community in North Trenton was almost always full of action. Liquor stores adorned every street corner, neighboring shops sold fried chicken and fish, and all of which were accompanied by persistent hustlers trying to sell you something. There were several barbershops and produce markets, and a handful of small churches. A few blocks south, there was a furniture warehouse, a gas station, and a milk machine. And there were more than a few boxing gyms, drawing in crowds of youngsters who wanted to learn a thing or two about fighting. It wasn't the shiniest part of town, by any means, but it was certainly vibrant.

Our home, which was nearly identical to all of the others, was a three-story brick building. When you first stepped through the front door, there was a modest living room, dining room, and kitchen. On the second floor there were three bedrooms and one bathroom. My oldest brother Eddie, who was more like Dad's shadow following him wherever he went, had one bedroom. My sisters Arlene and Paulette shared another. And my parents had the third. The attic on the third floor was where Dwight, Nate, and I slept.

As if our house wasn't already overcrowded, we also became the landing spot for folks who came to

Trenton from Virginia in search of new opportunities. Many of them came to work at Big Daddy's processing plant, and others were attracted to the plethora of jobs available that paid better than anything they could find back home. As they settled in and tried to find somewhere to live, they'd crash on our couches and floors for a few weeks at a time. We'd all gather together in the kitchen, laughing, talking, and listening to music. On Friday and Saturday evenings, when everyone was off from work, us kids were all sent upstairs and told not to come down. The adults would break out a deck of cards, turn the music up loudly, and dance all through the night.

It wasn't like our family had the means to support so many people. Sometimes, my parents were barely capable of keeping the lights on. In fact, there were a number of occasions where the power was out in our house for days while they scrambled to scrounge up enough cash to pay the electric bill.

Simply put, we didn't have much money. During the summer months, Mom would take me and my siblings to Chesterfield, a town about 25 minutes away from Trenton, to pick tomatoes. We'd get paid twenty-five cents per basket, and that money would go towards our school clothes for the upcoming school year.

A few weeks later, she would pack us all into the car, but this time, we'd drive to the Atlantic Mills Department Store. When we got there, my mom would go down by herself, leaving us alone to wait for her. She'd be gone for hours, picking out all of our clothes, two outfits for each kid. In that time, we'd fight, scream, cry, fall asleep, wake back up, and she'd still be gone.

Eventually, when we saw her walking back towards the car, a loaded cart full of her triumphs, we'd shoot up alert to give the impression that all had been copacetic while she'd been gone. After shoving all the bags into the trunk except for one, she'd get into the driver's seat, turn towards us with a big smile, and unveil our prize: a giant bag of buttery, artificially yellow popcorn. The hours-long ordeal of waiting for her was instantly worth it.

We may not have had a lot, but it sure taught us a lesson about gratitude and the value of hard work. They taught me that anything was possible if I had the audacity to want it. Besides the lawnmower I purchased that summer from selling produce with Uncle Cliff, I was also able to save up enough money to buy a bike. With the intention of delivering newspapers, I knew that my latest purchase would become yet another small ploy to make some pocket money. There was only one problem with my plan: no one in North Trenton bothered to pay the paperboy. I quickly abandoned that job. Instead, I returned to my initial jobs mowing people's lawns, shoveling their snow, and helping clean their yards. A year later, when I turned 12, my parents had finally saved up enough money to buy a bigger house. Our new place, which was in the much more affluent, middle-class neighborhood of Western Trenton, was a huge upgrade from our rowhouse. It was a three-story semi-detached house with six bedrooms and two bathrooms. For the first time ever, we had a front lawn, and a massive backyard for us to play in. There was a stairwell in the kitchen and another one in the living room, which meant you could get to the second floor from two different rooms in the house. I was fascinated with the whole thing.

Our new neighborhood was different, too. For one, there was grass everywhere. In North Trenton, it was all concrete and brick, and nature was a luxury we couldn't quite afford. But in Western Trenton, on Riverside Avenue where we lived, every home was surrounded by a luxurious, vibrant green lawn. Everywhere I turned, opportunity was flashing before my eyes. There were also far more working professionals here than in the north. In Western Trenton, doctors' and lawyers' offices lined the streets, instead of liquor stores, bars, and takeout restaurants. And there seemed to be far fewer people. We weren't all cramped into tiny spaces, sharing walls with our neighbors. One of Trenton's largest urban parks, Cadwalader Park, was close by, and my brother Nate and I would ride our bikes there sometimes, along with some of the other kids from the neighborhood.

I quickly discovered that Western Trenton was the perfect place to bring back my paper route. Here, not only did the residents pay me for delivering the newspaper, but they tipped me generously, especially around Christmas.

Riverside Avenue brought about considerable change for my family, altering the household dynamics in more ways than one. Shortly before we moved to our new house, Eddie graduated and got an apartment of his own. In his absence, my second oldest brother Kenny, who had been living in Virginia with my aunt since he was born, moved in with us. It was a strange shift, with the dynamics in the house shuffling to accommodate this new presence. He hadn't been raised with us, and suddenly being thrust into a house full of so much masculine energy was an adjustment, to say the least. But, moving into the bigger house certainly helped with the transition.

Kenny was a star athlete who had dreams of playing baseball in the big leagues, and had the talent to get there, too. I remember watching his games at the field near our house, in awe of the way the crowd reacted when he hit a home run, which he did well and often. I was so proud to call him my big brother, and just to be in proximity to him at all. But not everyone was on board with his goals. Dad, for one, didn't see things the way Kenny did. Unfortunately, his relationship with our dad was far shakier than it was with the rest of us, and the two butt heads often, and aggressively. To Dad, professional baseball wasn't a realistic dream. Instead, he wanted Kenny to get a regular job, like everyone else. Their volatile relationship caused so much friction and tension, I tried my best to avoid it at all costs.

As my family struggled to acclimate to our new living arrangement, I was having my own crisis. I didn't feel quite at home in this neighborhood, and I missed living close to my friends. In the beginning, I'd ride my bike all the way back to North Trenton, where I felt comfortable, and where I felt like I naturally fit in.

But after some time passed, I began to catch my stride on the west side, though it did take a little finessing. One day, I was heading out on my paper route, ready to collect my pay. As I casually rode my bike, one hand on the handle and the other scratching my chin, I thought about what I would spend the cash on. Maybe a new pair of shoes, I wondered, or a new record.

A few minutes later, I arrived at my location and confidently set out to collect my dues. As it turned out, two other boys had beaten me to the punch. They'd been going around, telling folks that they'd been the ones delivering the papers, and had been walking away with *my* money. I was furious. I knew that because I was new to the neighborhood, this was my time to establish myself, and to show the other kids what would happen if they messed with me.

I asked around for their names and quickly figured out who they were: Paul McRae and Greg Ross. As I rode my bike down the street, this time less casually, and with a more determined, intentional purpose. Eventually, I spotted them. I pulled up near the duo and confronted them about what they'd done. They laughed in my face, clearly unintimidated by who I was. What they didn't know was that I grew up with four older brothers. And if there was anything that experience taught me, it was that there was a cost to letting others walk all over you. If you let them get away with it the first time, there would most definitely be a second. That wasn't a risk I was willing to take. Plus, I'd been raised on the streets of North Trenton. There, you had to fight to protect your name. These boys clearly didn't know who they were messing with. Within a few minutes, I'd pushed both boys to the ground, thoroughly scaring them, took my money back, and established that I wasn't the one to fool with. I walked away proudly, feeling like I was on top of the world.

Unfortunately, those feelings didn't last for very long. At the time, I was in the ninth grade, about to graduate middle school. Unfortunately, I'd spent most of that year working hard to gain a reputation as a class clown, and not enough time paying attention in class. I was always talking over others, cracking jokes (sometimes at the expense of the teachers and other students), and just being disrespectful.

At the end of the year, our teacher Ms. Thomas handed out envelopes with our report cards inside. When she gave me mine, she looked at me with a glint of disappointment in her eyes. I brushed it off at first, grabbing my envelope jovially and stuffing it into my bag. Later that afternoon, as I was sitting in class, I pulled it out to see how I'd performed. As my eyes grazed the page, they landed on a big red F next to English. I stared at it, blinking my eyes closed, hoping it might disappear. Of course, it didn't. My mind whirled around in panic and disbelief.

How was this even possible? How could I fail English? After class, I walked up to Ms. Thomas and tried to convince her to change my mark. She looked at me, the flash of disappointment I saw before now glazing over her entire face. She shook her head, "no," And insisted that she wouldn't be changing anything. In her words, I'd gotten the mark I deserved.

I walked away despondently, realizing the magnitude of what had happened. If I failed English, that meant I wouldn't be graduating middle school. Walking home later that afternoon, with the report card burning a hole through my backpack, I thought about what I'd tell my parents. I didn't even know how to face them.

The thing was, I knew I was smart. I was most certainly smarter than a lot of the other kids in my class, kids who hadn't failed English. The other kids who hadn't failed to graduate middle school. So how'd I land myself in this position?

I thought back on all of the decisions I'd made, all of the times I'd sat thinking of a joke I could make to get the other kids to laugh, instead of listening to what the teacher was saying at the front of the class. I thought about all the days when I knew I was struggling, but brushed it off as a minor inconvenience, an inconsequential setback. I wished I could go back in time and force myself to do better. Obviously, I couldn't.

As I dragged my feet home, it dawned on me that the only aspect under my control was the present. I can't change what I've done, but I can control how I react. I can control *who I become.*

Chapter 2

The Heavy Days

For a lot of people, failure signifies defeat, a crippling reminder of one's limitations and shortcomings. I'm not one of those people. For me, failure is God granting me a do-over. It's an opportunity to try again, to face my challenges with wisdom, intentionality, and a sharpened understanding of consequences.

When I started high school in 1975, after nearly failing to graduate from middle school, I knew I had to change my trajectory. I'd spent all of ninth grade trying to become the class clown, to develop my identity as the funny guy. While I'd succeeded, at least in that respect, in the end, the joke was on me. When I entered the tenth grade, I had to retake ninth grade English, which meant that when all of the other students were heading home for the day, I was still stuck in class. I'd sit by the window, watching all of my friends pile onto the bus, wishing I could join them. As the smell of diesel filled the air every afternoon, the yellow buses bouncing away from the schoolyard, I was reminded of my dire reality: I was beginning my high school career already two steps behind my peers.

It was humiliating, but it also instilled in me a sense of urgency, a determination to get my life on track. I wasn't about to let 'the guy who failed middle school' define how everyone else saw me. I approached my English teacher and laid it all out for him, all of my weaknesses, and where I struggled most. This time around, I wouldn't settle for a passing grade, I was set on achieving excellence.

That resolve began to extend far beyond English class. I knew that at the end of every semester, the school announced the names of the students who'd made the honor roll, and it was my mission to make it on that list; to prove to myself and everyone else that I could do it. My failure ripped open a competitive streak that had been lying dormant inside me. I was a bull, and the thought of letting my potential go to waste was the red flag provoking me into a furious rush towards success.

Though I found myself with a renewed determination to do well in school, my desires weren't exactly academically inclined. It wasn't that I suddenly understood the value of education, or that I gained a deeper love for learning. I just wanted to prove myself. What most excited me was an education in trades. My school had a vocational wing, and I was committed to taking full advantage of it. I completed the exploratory program that summer, where I was able to get a feel for the different options available to me. From carpentry and masonry to sheet metal, the options were endless. While I relished every moment, I ended the program with a clear focus in mind: auto mechanics.

I grew up in a car-obsessed household. My dad would often regale us with tales of his younger days, racing cars with his brothers and friends in Virginia. Everyone in my family – from my father and my brothers to uncles and cousins – all loved being around, underneath, and inside cars. My cousin Harrison and my brother Eddie both owned high-performance Chevy vehicles, so from a young age, I'd gained an intimate understanding of things like engine size and horsepower. Dad's brother was also a mechanic, mostly on farming equipment, but he also worked on cars and trucks, too. Both he and Dad were usually out tinkering with one of the family's many cars and trucks. Whenever I had the chance, I'd be out there with them, asking non-stop questions about what they were doing, handing them tools, or getting my hands dirty helping out.

Years before entering high school, I was already very familiar with the inner workings of vehicles. I knew how to do an oil change, and had been swapping out flat tires since I was in elementary school. I could also identify almost every car on the road. In short, auto mechanics was a no brainer. Cars – their maintenance, health and upkeep – were in my blood; a passion that bonded me to my family. And I had a natural propensity for it, too. I was always good at working with my hands which allowed me to maneuver my way around the insides of a car almost instinctively.

In the vocational wing, auto mechanics was separated into two distinct classes: small engines (stuff like motorcycles, motorboats, lawnmowers and other outdoor power equipment) with Mr. DiMaggio, and cars with Mr. Baron. The two teachers were as different and distinct as the engines they worked on. Mr. DiMaggio was meticulous about his appearance and the way he presented himself. His hair was always styled neatly, and he wore an apron over his clothes to ensure they didn't get dirty while working on repairs. He was articulate, light-hearted, and I found him very easy to talk to, so we got along quite well.

Mr. Baron, on the other hand, was a true mechanic – elbow deep in the dirt and grease. He wore a blue mechanic's jumpsuit, which was often black from the oil, and he didn't spend too much time concerned with how he looked. His personality was as rough as his appearance. He wasn't one for many words, and he didn't tolerate any nonsense. If you were taking his class, you had to be prepared to work hard and listen intently, because he wasn't going to repeat himself.

I had a good rapport with both teachers, and they often gave me bigger and tougher assignments, especially Mr. Baron. While other students were doing oil changes, he had me taking engines apart, removing transmissions and doing brake jobs. When it came to auto mechanics, I was on top of the pecking order. I quickly gained a reputation in the vocational wing for my exceptional skills. There, I wasn't recognized in relation to my older brothers. I had developed an identity separate from my family. I was just John, not Dwight or Nate or Kenny or Eddie's younger brother. I was able to establish my own persona, to be my own man (well, almost).

The same can't be said for the rest of school, where I pretty much faded into the crowd. I attended a predominantly Black school with about 3,000 students. Unlike my brothers, who'd all been star athletes, I didn't really gravitate to sports. So, if anyone recognized me from my family name or in relation to one of my brothers, they were pretty quickly disappointed when they discovered how different from them I'd turned out to be. I may have been highly competent in trades, but socially, I was lacking. And that shortfall was ever more apparent when it came to girls. I had no idea how to talk to them, flirt, or buff my personality to make myself more appealing. I was often a bumbling mess, tripping over my own words, awkwardly chattering away until they found an excuse to stop talking to me.

It wasn't an ideal scenario. Like most high school boys, I was eager to meet girls, but instead I found myself in competition with jocks from the basketball and football teams. They got all of the attention from the girls and were intent on letting everyone else in school know that they were at the top of the food chain. I wasn't an athlete, which contributed to my status as persona non grata. It also made me someone the jocks initially thought they could project their hypermasculinity onto – someone they could make an example of. But with four older brothers, I was used to that kind of posturing, and I knew that the worst thing I could do was to cow tail to their bullying tactics.

One day, when I was in gym class, a boy named Mark Anthony was mouthing off, being disrespectful to some of the guys, including me. He was around my size, just a little bit shorter. It was clear he was trying to position himself as a tough guy, and as someone the others should be afraid of, but not me. At one point, hoping to make the point really clear, he pushed me. Little did he know, he chose the wrong one. I wasn't about to let him cement *his* reputation *at my expense*. Forcefully, I hit him back, and he fell back into the lockers. A mixture of gasps and chuckles rose from my classmates. Mark pushed himself back up and tried to brush it off like nothing had happened. Following that incident, and for the most part, the guys at school realized I wasn't someone they could push around. It didn't mean they liked me any more than before, they just no longer viewed me as an easy target.

Despite how it may have seemed, I was actually pretty content with my social life. I hung out in the vocational wing most of the time anyway. And after school, that was when things really got exciting.

There was a playground and basketball court on Edgewood Avenue, a few blocks from where my family lived. Every day, I would go there to meet my friends and we'd play ball or sit around talking smack to each other. Among the regular attendees were my best friend Michael and my sister Paulette's boyfriend, George. George came from the Goodman family, who were also from Virginia. When they first moved north to Trenton, they stayed at our home for a while until they secured their own dwellings in the neighborhood. Our families had stayed close throughout the years, even after Paulette got pregnant in high school with George's baby.

One day, me, Michael, George, and our other friend Ricky were hanging out on the court, playing two on two basketball. Michael and I played on one team, George and Ricky on the other. At one point, I tossed Michael the ball and began running forward, covering George. But after catching the ball, Mike just stood there, staring at something behind me. I turned around to see what he was looking at. That's when I noticed a large man walking on the court towards us, smiling. He was around 6'3, 300 lbs, and he was dressed well, with a large gold chain dangling shamelessly from the open collar of his shirt.

"Hey boys, how you doin'?" he asked us, casually. We all looked at each other, a little hesitantly. The man told us his name was Jackie Ellis, though some people called him Big 12. He told us that he managed a group of artists called the TNJs (who would later become the well-known disco band Instant Funk). He pointed to a building down the street from the basketball court which had once been an oil and coal business called Tattersol, but had been sitting vacant for some time now. Jackie had just bought the place and was turning it into a social club, somewhere we could hang out if we wanted to.

Our interest was piqued. He told us to come with him inside, and that he'd give us a tour. Perhaps naively, we followed. It was like something out of a movie – definitely not like any place I'd ever been to. It was a large office space which was in the process of being converted to a club. As he walked around, he shared his vision with us. In the large main room, there would be pool tables scattered throughout, booths for people to sit, and a large bar in the corner, with colored lights illuminating the room with a subtle red glow. He also pointed out the other separate rooms where lounging beds and couches would eventually line the walls. Over the next few weeks, we helped Jackie with the renovations. And when it was time to open up, he let us hang around as much as we wanted.

The club was called the Total Experience. And that's precisely what it was. In a way, it became a second school for me. But instead of learning math and English, here I got an education on life, and more specifically, the streets.

Every day after school, Mike (who was a year older than me) and I would meet at the basketball court, play for a little while, then head inside the club. I was only 15 at the time and certainly too young to be hanging out there. As we passed more and more of our time at the Total Experience, it became clear that the club wasn't just a spot to hang out "socially." It was a place for folks to indulge in any and all of their vices. And Jackie was way more than a businessman.

George's older brother Johnny told us that Jackie was a notorious drug dealer who'd previously served time in prison for murder. Initially, it was shocking because Jackie was such a pleasant presence to be around. He was always generous and personable with us, and not at all like the image I'd concocted in my head of how an infamous drug kingpin would behave. But over time, my perception of him evolved, and I was able to see past his 'nice guy' persona.

At Total Experience, I routinely watched Jackie's guys cutting up cocaine on the tables, weighing it on small electronic scales, and scooping it into little plastic baggies. Sex workers, many of whom also sold drugs for Jackie, were usually lounging around in one of the club's many rooms, or even putting on live sex shows. Although Jackie didn't permit the actual selling of drugs in the club, it still happened on many occasions. I saw stacks of cash passed from hand to hand, as drug dealers conducted their trade under the glow of the club's lights. Sometimes, I'd catch a glimpse of the pistol tucked into Jackie's trousers, and a shiver would run through me.

This was a completely different world than anything I'd ever been exposed to. I came from a pretty strait-laced household. Drugs, sex, gambling; these things were all foreign to me. Perhaps because of my stricter and more conventional upbringing, I was able to process what I saw at Total Experience with a more keen, discerning eye than some of the other young guys who hung out there with us.

While they only saw the ease with which drug dealers were able to make money,, I saw a more holistic picture. My eyes couldn't gloss over the darkness of addiction or the hollowing impact drugs had on its users. I witnessed the desperation of many of the club's patrons, the urgency etched into the contours of their faces as they slapped their weekly earnings into the palm of someone who'd slip them a small plastic bag in exchange.

I also got a front-row seat to the violence that walked hand-in-hand with the drug trade; particularly when you worked for Jackie. One night, one of the sex workers who sold drugs for him walked into the club with her head lowered and a darkness eclipsing her eyes. She was there delivering her earnings to Jackie, who grabbed the stack of money from her, instantly recognizing that it was short of what he'd expected. Without saying a word, he dragged her to the canal behind the club and pushed her head into the murky water, a brutal baptism of sorts. As her hair floated on the surface, her body thrashing violently as she struggled for breath, the whole place went silent. There were very real, very painful consequences for pissing Jackie off.

On another occasion, Jackie had sent one of his guys, a man named Nixon, to New York to pick up some drugs for him. When Nixon returned, he was feeling a little braggadocious about having gone to the big apple. He strutted around the club, boasting about everything he'd done. Jackie, who happened to be in New York at the same time, had watched him cop the drugs, and apparently, Nixon hadn't gone alone. He'd taken a friend with him, something that Jackie had no tolerance for.

After watching Nixon shoot his mouth off for a few minutes, Jackie calmly got up and walked towards him. He grabbed him by the neck and tossed him like a bag of rice into another room. He beat Nixon viciously, throwing him around as though he were a weightless, inanimate object. I never had any desire to get involved in drug dealing, and the more I watched incidents like this unfold, the further it increased my disdain for the whole thing. Many of the other young guys who spent time at Total Experience wanted to participate in the things they saw happening. I, on the other hand, was just happy to observe. The extent of my involvement was limited to drinking beer and smoking a little bit of weed – both of which I tried for the first time at the club. But I always knew when it was time to check myself, and roll back the indulgence to a place that felt safe.

Still, regardless of how rough and merciless I saw Jackie behaving towards others, he never projected that violence onto me or Mike. He recognized that neither of us were cut out for that kind of lifestyle, and he encouraged us to stay out of trouble, and to pursue more upstanding, lawful endeavors. He always told us to stay in school, and to focus on getting good grades. He also told us he was proud of us, something I wasn't really used to hearing from any of the other adults in my life.

It was unconventional, but Jackie became one of the first mentors I've ever had. He taught me how to conduct myself in life and in business, and how to use words tactfully to get further along. Despite the violent and criminal path he'd chosen, he had a keen and strategic mind. He schooled me on how to sniff out who was a tough guy and who was really a chump, but especially how to sharpen my discernment when it came to my interactions with others. It's a skill that helped me throughout all arenas of my life, not just on the streets. He trained me and Mike in boxing techniques and would give us lessons on defending ourselves. Though I'd already had my fair share of fights in life, Jackie's lessons reiterated to me the importance of standing up for myself. I wouldn't say I followed his example exactly, since he had a nasty temper and a lust for violence, traits I didn't share or even like. But I learned things about life and people that I may not have gained otherwise.

I saw firsthand that even the people who appeared as tough guys, the hustlers hanging around on the streets who stoked fear into anyone who passed by, answered to someone else. They had their own sources of terror. For most of them, that happened to be Jackie. There was a man we called Bones who worked with Jackie at the club and also ran his own taxi and limo service. Sometimes when we arrived at the club in the evenings, Jackie would climb into the back of the white Lincoln limo and beckon us to join him. Bones would drive around the city and Jackie would point out who all of the street hustlers were before pulling up to them and jacking their cash. Robbing people was actually something that Jackie did often. It seemed like a strange hobby to me, especially since he didn't need what he was taking. But it was a power move. He robbed them because he could, and in turn, it asserted his dominance over everyone else.

One evening, when Jackie was feeling particularly untouchable, he said that he wanted to go to Trenton's gambling hall which we called the Crap's House. As a bunch of us played pool, Jackie stood on one corner of the table, telling us what he had in mind.

"We're going to go to the Crap's House," he said, pausing to take a sip of his drink before continuing. "We're going to gamble. And if we lose, we're going to rob it." The guys all burst out laughing, dapping him up and voicing their approval. Mike and I exchanged nervous glances. We already knew we weren't included in this scheme, but it was such a bold move that I couldn't help but admire him a little. I watched on as they quickly put together a plan. They had what we call a puzzle – a disassembled shotgun. Every person would take one piece of the puzzle. If, by the end of the night, the gambling wasn't successful, they'd step outside and put all of the pieces together. A few hours later, they came back to the club with an assembled shotgun and a bag full of cash.

Months passed this way, with Mike and me spending nearly every evening at the Total Experience. It was basically my second home at this point. Still, in all the time I spent going to the club, I only broke my curfew one time. On that particular night, Jackie had instructed the bartender, Walt, not to charge anyone money for drinks. The club didn't have a liquor license, and he'd gained intel that they'd be visited by some undercover cops.

"When we open up those doors tonight, you don't take a single penny for any drink, you got that? If a guy wants a beer, you give him a beer," Jackie reiterated for probably the tenth time. Well, at some point during the night, a man approached the bar, asked for a beer and proceeded to pull out $2... and a badge. Within minutes, cops stormed into the club, yelling at everyone to clear out. Jackie had been fast asleep in one of the rooms when the chaos started, waking him up. He walked into the main room of the club, his eyes still cloudy with sleep, and asked what all the commotion was. One of the cops approached Jackie cautiously.

"Mr. Ellis, we're raiding the place because you're selling liquor without a license." Jackie shook his head, laughing. After explaining to him that they were taking him into the precinct for questioning, we all stood outside with Jackie on the curb as he gave us instructions to close down the club and wait for him. Then, one of the officers turned to Jackie, his voice low and wary.

"Mr. Ellis, can we cuff you?" he asked, pulling out the silver handcuffs from his holster and holding them out sheepishly. I watched the scene unfold, bewildered. It was one thing to see some of the gangsters on the streets offer their respects to Jackie. But I was shocked to see cops dispense that same degree of esteem (or perhaps it was simply fear, sometimes it's hard to tell the difference).

After locking up the club, Mike and I headed inside with some of Jackie's other men to wait for him. Two hours later, he was back. As we all gathered around to listen to his story about what went down, I caught a glimpse of the clock hanging on the wall behind him. It was nearly morning, and I had long-since broken my curfew. A steady surge of fear coursed through me. To quell my anxiety, I told myself that if I made it home after my dad left for work, he might not even realize that I'd never come home. I nudged Mike, nodding my head towards the clock, and I saw the same fear I was experiencing work its way through him, too.

We told Jackie we had to leave and ran out the door. We hopped on our bikes and peddled home as quickly as we could, both unsure of what would happen to the other, but too fearful for ourselves to really care. "Dad will be gone for work already," I told myself. "It's going to be fine. They probably didn't even notice."

Boy was I wrong. When I pulled up to the front of the house, Dad pushed open the front door with fury and fear etched into his face.

"Boy, where the hell have you been?" he shouted, grabbing me by the collar of my shirt. By this point in my life, my dad had pretty much stopped with corporal punishment. Though it had been a regular and routine part of my childhood, we both knew I'd outgrown the force of his hand. Still, he wasn't about to let me get away with this violation without consequences. After dragging me inside, and unleashing a verbal lashing, he told me I was grounded for one month. That meant that other than going to school, I had to keep my butt at home all day, every day. I wasn't even allowed to ride my bike. Mike, as it turned out, received the same punishment.

I later returned to the club to tell Jackie what had happened. Admirably, he felt compelled to come to my defense. He came by the house and spoke with my parents, explaining to them what had happened, and taking responsibility for my tardiness. He promised them that it wouldn't happen again.

"If I see him at the club past curfew, I'll beat his ass for you myself," he laughed, shaking Dad's hand. Jackie's words hadn't done anything to change my punishment, but I was honored that he'd even stopped by.

After that, I began spending less time at Total Experience. It wasn't only that I'd been grounded and simply couldn't spend my evenings there, but I also started a new job which altered my availability. Dad had gotten me a position at National Waste for the summer and winter breaks, where he worked collecting trash. He expected all of us to work and contribute to the household in some capacity, so a lot of the money I made went straight to his pocket, not mine. There were no negotiations or conversations about this. If we wanted to live in his house, we had to work, and we had to contribute, no questions asked. On at least one occasion, my dad actually collected and cashed my check from work before I even had a chance to see it. His authoritarianism when it came to employment and money drove most of my brothers out of the house. By this time, they'd all finished school and had started working. Instead of handing over half their money to Dad every week, they'd all decided that independence, both financial and personal, seemed like a better bargain. Still, my father let me keep some of my money, so I didn't really mind. Plus, I kind of liked my job.

I worked on the back of garbage trucks, picking up trash cans and unloading them into the back. I was assigned to a route in Burlington County, around 25 miles away from Trenton. The neighborhoods I worked in were very suburban, very wealthy, and very white. The houses were massive, and the grass was greener than any I'd ever seen before. And there was so much space between the houses, it made West Trenton, which was one of the nicer areas of the city, seem overcrowded. I quickly discovered how entitled rich people could be. As many times as we reminded them not to put their dog poop on top of the bags, every week when I showed up, there it was, a smelly gift waiting for me.

But I learned how to deal with it. In fact, I spent the bulk of my time at National Waste learning on my feet. I'd barely received any training, so I had to figure out most things on my own. No one instructed me how to hold onto the back of the truck, when to jump off or how to lift and dump the trash into the back. I watched the other guys I worked with, and eventually came up with my own style to maximize efficiency. As the truck moved from house to house, I'd keep up a steady jog. Within a few weeks of work, I'd leaned out significantly. As my body changed with the pace of the work, I gained a new appreciation for athleticism and how it made me feel.

I was only 16 when I started working there, and all of the other guys I worked with were much older. They clowned me a lot about my experience with women, which at that time was pitiful and nearly non-existent. But they gave me advice and even tried to teach me how to talk to girls and flirt. They shared stories about their own hits and misses and I listened on in amazement.

As the summer came to an end, I entered the 11th grade with a renewed sense of confidence. It wasn't only because of my new athletic build or the fact that I'd spent the last year and a half being mentored by one of the city's biggest gangsters. I had something else that helped me stand out from the crowd: a car. I'd been able to save up enough cash to buy a 68 Ford Torino for $200. I cherished that thing like it was my baby. Now, I drove myself to school instead of catching the bus with the rest of the kids. I felt like I was finally moving on up in the world. And the girls seemed to take notice a lot more, too.

That year, I befriended two twin sisters, Arlene and Darlene, and their friend Doreen. Every day, the three of them would ask me to go to lunch with them, and we'd hop in my car and drive somewhere nearby to eat. It never really dawned on me that they were using me to drive them around. And truthfully, even if I'd noticed, it probably wouldn't have made any difference. These girls were downright beautiful, and I was just happy to be spending time with them. Regardless of how our friendship started, we grew to be quite close. I began branching out and making more friends, too. I wasn't popular by any means, but I got along with everyone, and everyone got along with me.

That year, I got a new afterschool job at Firestone, something that better aligned with my passions and interests. There, I would change tires, do oil changes, and work on minor repairs. It felt like everything in my life was falling into place. Most of my days were spent working on cars both at school and at work, and the rest of my time was spent studying and spending time with the people I loved. By the time the school year came to an end, I felt truly untouchable.

I had my own money, my own car, and a solid group of friends. Additionally, for the second year in a row, I'd managed to make the honor roll. I was flying high. By the time 12th grade rolled around, I felt like my life could only get better from there. Little did I know, something insidious and life-changing was waiting for me just around the corner.

In September of 1977, I was 17 and just beginning my final year of high school. From the jump, things seemed to be going well. Mr. Baron had grown to trust my skills immensely, and he even let me do some big repairs on the principal's car. I felt confident in the direction I was going, and that I had the kind of skills to turn my passion into a career down the line. At that time, I was considering becoming a truck driver, like Dad. Even though I was older now, and had met more people and had more experiences in life, my dad was still my hero. He was still the man I looked up to the most. Over the years, as I grew from a young boy to a young man, our relationship evolved steadily. Now, instead of watching him work on his trucks, I actively helped him. I even knew some tricks and strategies that he didn't.

My life at home was quieter than it had been growing up. Most of my siblings had grown up and moved out, so it was only Mom, Dad, Arlene and me still there. Don't get me wrong, the others still came by often to visit, but our day-to-day life had slowed from a constant rolling boil to a quiet simmer. An aura of stillness settled over everything. Our meals were no longer loud spectacles, with my brothers fighting over the last piece of bacon, or all of us sharing stories about our days around the dinner table. Instead, Arlene and I would usually throw something together quickly and eat, just the two of us, while we did our homework.

At first, we thought Mom was just tired. She'd spent our entire lives running the household, so it made sense that she took advantage of this newfound freedom, where she didn't have a house full of kids pulling her every which way. But eventually, it became clear that something wasn't right. Some days, she was too exhausted to even get out of bed and she'd spend the entire afternoon and evening laying in bed with the curtains drawn. This was completely out of character for her. Mom had always been active, both physically and socially. She had a large and varied circle of friends, and was one of the leading members of a woman's organization that regularly put on charity fundraisers and community events. She was the kind of woman that could command the attention of an entire room just by stepping into it, with her presence drawing people like magnets to metal. I'm sure many people think that about their mothers, that they are the most spectacular people on the planet. But Mom was the real deal. Everyone who knew her loved her.

For my whole life, Mom went to the salon once a week to get her hair done. Often, she and my sisters would go together. They all had thick black locks, and Mom would get hers tinted with golden brown highlights, a color that accentuated her complexion perfectly. But in those days, she was barely getting out of the house at all, let alone to get her hair done. It was a strange shift to witness, and both Arlene and I didn't understand what was going on with her.

One day, when Arlene and I were hanging out at home, Dad walked into the room and switched off the TV set. He told us that he needed to talk to us about something important. We shot each other nervous glances, unsure of what to expect.

"You've probably noticed Mom isn't really herself these days," he said, rubbing his chin with his hand, a subtle shake in his voice. "Well, she's sick. Mom is very sick. She... she has cancer."

Arlene cried out a pain-laced shriek. I gasped, staring hard at Dad's face, searching for answers. I didn't know too much about cancer, but I knew it was deadly. I knew that it certainly wasn't something you wanted your mom to be diagnosed with. He explained to us that this was the reason she'd been so tired lately, so emotionally and physically distant. We listened quietly, Arlene sobbing into her hands. We needed to help out around the house more, he told us, to help make her life as comfortable as possible. We nodded.

"Dad," Arlene asked, her face wet with tears, "is mom going to die?" Dad stayed silent for a minute, staring hard into the distance.

"The doctors aren't confident she's going to make it. They say she probably has six months." I just sat there, trembling, shock and terror moving through me like poison. I couldn't fathom a world without my mom. She'd been everything to me, to all of us. She was the one who took care of us, both physically and emotionally. She ran the whole household. I felt certain that without her, our entire lives would fall apart.

I tried to spend as much time with her as I could. Whenever I came home from school or work, I'd go lay next to her in her bed. She'd tell me to go outside, to go find me a girlfriend and start living my life. I could both feel and see her fading away, detaching herself from us slowly. It was then that I began to understand the magnitude of her disease and the intensity of its impact. I was watching Mom deteriorate before my eyes; her hair falling out in large, terrifying clumps, her skin slowly graying.

But I still had hope that her physicians were wrong. They'd given her six months to live, but I'd heard stories about people outliving the death sentences given to them by their doctors. Mom would be one of those people, I was sure; she'd make it through. We were living through a terrible nightmare and when it was all over, we'd laugh about the doctors who'd foolishly underestimated my mother.

Over the next few months, Mom's condition worsened and her illness became something that permeated into my every waking thought. As I sat in class, or worked on an assignment in the mechanics department, I wondered about her, how she was feeling, *if she was still alive*. If I wasn't at home next to her, I wanted to be.

During this time, our house was rarely empty. Mom had so many friends, so many people who loved her, and there was always someone there checking on her. One evening, a few months after her initial diagnosis, my brother Dwight and sister Paulette were at the house visiting. Mom's pain had increased to an unmanageable intensity, and we watched her writhe in agony. Dad called an ambulance who quickly sped over to the house and checked her vitals. She wasn't doing well. They placed her on a stretcher and carried her frail body to the back of the ambulance and loaded her inside. I was terrified, and I couldn't stop my hands from shaking. At the same time, I couldn't look away, my eyes locked on my Mom's face; darkened and distorted by her suffering.

After admitting my mom to the hospital that day, she never returned home. Every day after school, I'd go to the hospital to visit her. And each time I walked into her room, I was pained at her appearance. She had oxygen tubes in her nose and all of the color had seeped out of her face. She looked weaker and weaker by the minute. I couldn't bear to see her that way, the life fading from her body like light from a winter sky. But I still had this innocent hope that her condition would turn around. I clung to it, desperately, as if the hope itself was going to save her.

On Valentine's Day, I was in my room at home when I heard the phone ring. As I headed down the stairs, I heard a horrible wail and froze. Dad was on the phone, bawling like a little boy. He just kept repeating 'I love you Delores,' over and over again. After a minute, he slammed the receiver down and ran towards the front door. He paused, seeing me standing there on the stairs, and nodded his head. He said he was going to the hospital and ran out the door.

He didn't have to say it. I knew that it had happened, the moment we'd all been dreading. I could barely stand, both my own body and the ground beneath me like jelly. I held onto the banister and lowered myself down. I sat there on the stairs, my face in my hands, and sobbed hysterically.

Mom was gone. I'd never hear her infectious laugh again, never see her beaming smile. She'd never cook me her famous mac n' cheese or bake me a chocolate cake when I was having a bad day. I'd never feel her arms wrap around me, squeezing me in a warm embrace. I'd never get to talk to her about relationships or girls. She wouldn't be at my graduation, or my wedding. She'd never meet my kids. The immensity of my loss hit me in stages, in chunks of paralyzing misery. My grief was multifaceted, somehow both emotional and physical. I felt the pain of her absence in my body, like a phantom limb. Everything reminded me of her. I kept thinking to myself how ironic it was that the only person I wanted to talk to about my sadness was the one person I'd never get a chance to talk to again.

Her funeral came and went in a blur; in a haze of tears and memories. My siblings and I all huddled together, holding each other, and trying to process the reality we were facing that we'd have to go on living without her. Dad struggled even more than we did. For the first time in my life, he wasn't that strong guy who could deal with anything. For weeks, I'd walk by his bedroom and hear him wailing. His grief was something so heavy and palpable, I felt like I could touch it and hold it in my hand. It was strange and terribly sad, watching the strongest person I knew crumble into a tearful wreck every evening.

My youngest sister Arlene, who'd been very close to our mother, was also having an especially hard time. She was far too young to be forced to navigate life without a mom. I tried to watch out for her as much as I could, but I was also grappling with my own loss and unmanageable grief.

For the first few weeks following Mom's death, many of her old friends would come to the house to check on us, to make sure we were doing alright. All of our neighbors stopped by to offer their condolences, to drop off food, and share with us how much Mom had meant to them. It became apparent how much of an impact she'd had on everyone she interacted with.

Even though most of my siblings had moved out of the house, we all grew a lot closer after Mom's death. It was almost like, because she was gone, we had to cling even more desperately to each other and to our memories of her. We spoke often, checking up on each other, taking turns talking to each other through the ebbs and flows of our collective grief.

For the next few months, going through life felt like walking through water. I was going through the motions, attending my classes, working, and preparing to close out my high school career. But everything felt heavy, weighed down by the enormously tender reality that nothing would ever be the same again. As my high school graduation approached, I tried to steady myself, to prepare to wade through the rest of my life without her by my side.

Chapter 3

When a Boy Becomes a Man

In 1978, a few months after Mom's death, I walked across the stage at my high school graduation. It was a bittersweet day, both celebratory and sad. After a shaky start, having to repeat ninth grade English, I'd earned a spot on the honor roll, and was in the top ten percentile of a graduating class of 600 kids. I proved to myself and everyone else that I was capable of accomplishing anything I put my mind to. And yet the one person who I desperately wanted to reveal the fruits of my labor to was absent.

I knew Mom would be proud of me, that she was there with me in spirit. But when I stood on the stage, looking out at the sea of faces, all I wanted was to see hers beaming back at me, with her golden smile and loud, sunny laugh. Experiencing her death was an exercise in survival and growth; losing Mom taught me lessons about life no school, no teacher, and no book could have ever provided. It also taught me that life treks forward, no matter what you're going through, and that you'll never appreciate anyone as much as when they're gone. As the rest of my class hugged their mothers and snapped pictures with them side by side, I swallowed the lump of grief at the back of my throat and tried to hide my envy. I'd never get the chance to celebrate life with Mom again.

It was still a happy day, don't get me wrong. Dad was there, and my sisters, too. My cousin Dwight was in my graduating class, so some of my extended family showed up for the occasion, as well. My brothers couldn't make it to the ceremony, but afterwards we all headed back to the house and my sisters cooked us up a feast. Surrounded by loved ones, we shared a meal, exchanged thoughts about the future, and danced the night away.

Even though I had stellar grades, my plan had always been to be a mechanic. I never envisioned myself pursuing a career that didn't involve being elbows deep in the engine of a car. Auto mechanics was my life's passion. When I was fixing a car, my hands coated in black oil, I felt like a surgeon investigating the diseased guts of my patient, searching for the root of the problem. It was a simple and pure process: diagnose the problem, find the solution, execute. Fixing cars was uncomplicated and straightforward; a language I was fluent in.

After graduating, I got a job at Haldeman Ford, a dealership not too far from where I lived. My job there was just doing minor repairs like oil changes and rotating tires, as well as prepping new cars for delivery. One of my favorite roles at the dealership was to park the new cars as they came in off of the trucks. I was

John E. Harmon Sr. IOM

one of the first people to drive the cars, and the feeling of the shiny leather steering wheel in my hands was exhilarating. I was still such a young guy, but being in such close proximity to brand new cars made me feel important.

Every day after work, I'd head over to Mercer County Community College, where my friends and I played intramural or pick up basketball. The gym was huge and had four basketball courts so we'd either break off into two big teams and play full court or separate into smaller groups and use the half courts instead. Even though I wasn't a student at Mercer, I became a popular fixture on campus as a face most people would probably recognize because of how often I was there.

One day, I was walking to the gym when I was stopped by three older Black women who worked at the college. Even though I didn't know their names, they were well aware of mine. I later learned that their names were Voncile Emmons, Martha Baker, and Martha Gunning. "John," Ms. Voncile, the tallest of the three said, looking at me with a serious look on her face, "you're not a student here, are you?"

"No ma'am," I said, shifting the basketball underneath my arm.

"And why not? You're always here anyway. You might as well just enroll and make something of yourself," Martha Gunning said with a face full of freckles. She seemed to be the oldest of the bunch. I tried my best to explain to them that I didn't really see myself going to college, and that I had alternative life plans. But they didn't seem convinced one bit, and one of the Martha's grabbed me by the elbow and guided me toward the office.

When we got there, they sat me down and began asking me questions about what subjects I enjoyed and what I would major in if I were to go to school. I thought about it for a minute, and then responded with business. I'd heard of other people getting business degrees and it seemed interesting enough. Plus, it seemed like a major that could be easily applied to real world opportunities. Before I even knew what was happening, they grabbed a stack of applications from a registration table and had me fill them out. Over the next few weeks, they assisted with SAT preparation, set me up to complete the placement exam, and helped me fill out grant applications.

Within no time, I received a letter in the mail, with Mercer College's green and gold insignia stamped on the front. I held it in my hands as if it was something fragile and precious, before ripping it open to reveal the paper inside. As the envelope dropped to the ground, my eyes scanned the page. I was accepted into the business administration program.

I walked around that day feeling a little dazed. I had never even considered going to college before. It wasn't that I couldn't go, I'd just never factored it into my plans for the future. I'd always been surrounded by blue-collar workers; people who worked with their hands, or did manual or trade-related labor. When I looked at my family, my friends, and even my neighbors, I couldn't think of a single person who had attended college. Perhaps I had subconsciously confined myself to a world where I felt comfortable operating in. Many others, including my dad and my brothers, had walked the same path before me so I hadn't really thought about charting a course of my own. But now, thanks to Ms. Voncile, and the Marthas, I was imagining a world of possibilities that had never crossed my mind before. It almost seemed surreal that, soon, I'd be a college student.

Upon receiving my acceptance letter, Martha Baker helped me pick out my classes for my first and second semesters. Once everything was confirmed, I began sharing the news. Dad was happy for me, and he reminded me more than once that Mom would have been very proud, too. My friends were all surprised, but they slapped me on the back and congratulated me anyway.

When I told the guys I worked with at Haldeman Ford, who were mostly older, rough-around-the-edges white guys who'd been mechanics for most of their lives, they kind of chuckled and rolled their eyes. "College boy, huh?" one of them quipped, laughing as though I'd just told them I was on my way to Hollywood. I felt a sting of pain as I hadn't anticipated such an icy response, or for them to look at me with so much resentment. I sensed they didn't believe I was up to the task, like maybe they thought I was punching higher than my weight class. Either way, I left work that afternoon feeling even more motivated to prove myself and perform well. I couldn't give them the satisfaction of being right.

When I began school that year, in 1979, I felt like I was really coming into myself. Even though I'd been nervous at first, unsure if advanced education was really what I wanted to do, I quickly settled into my new life as a college student. I spent most of my days juggling classes, homework, basketball, and work. The evenings were reserved for studying mostly, but I balanced that with a healthy dose of nightly outings.

Shortly before I started at Mercer, I'd reconnected with a childhood friend named Kevin, who lived nearby. We played basketball and shot pool together between my classes. I have him to thank for helping me evade the dreaded freshman fifteen. He was in excellent shape, and we'd go for runs together. He pushed me physically, teaching me a valuable lesson about using the power of your mind to control your body. He was also a boxer so he taught me how to accurately throw a punch, and how to swivel my hips to maximize the power of my strikes. We spent a lot of time together in those days. His parents were divorced and he stayed with his mother, Alma, who we all called Big Al. Big Al took on the role of second mother to me, offering the warm, nurturing environment I craved so much at the time. I'd join Kevin and his family at Big Al's for Sunday dinner where she'd make an impressive spread of oxtail and gravy, collard greens and rice, mac n' cheese, and a deep-dish apple pie for dessert. I always ate well at Big Al's.

After dinner, Kevin and I would get ready to go to the weekly dance party at BT's Lounge. The space usually had an older crowd during the weekdays, but Sundays were for the youngins. And we showed up in droves, dressed to the nines in our sharpest suits and shiniest shoes, ready to bring our best moves to the dance floor. From 9 p.m. to 2 a.m. on Sundays, BT's was the place to be.

When it closed, we'd all pile out and head to the afterhours club to keep the party going. Kevin and I especially liked a spot called Mr. P's which opened at 2 a.m., and stayed open until the sun came up. It was a tiny, cramped joint with a small bar and a smoky dance floor that stayed jam packed. The music at Mr. P's was what had us coming back every week. He played everything from The Temptations and The O'Jays to Marvin Gaye. This was also around the time when rap music was first developing, so when Kurtis Blow's voice rang out of the speakers, ordering us to clap our hands, the dance floor erupted in celebration.

One Sunday, after already breaking a sweat at BT's, Kevin and I pulled up at Mr. P's, ready to keep the party going. I was driving Dad's 77' Cadillac Fleetwood Brougham with beige leather guts, chrome spinners, and white wall tires. The vehicle itself was a showstopper, and my impressive driving skills only increased the appeal. I pulled up fast, and deftly backed up into a parking spot, putting on a bit of a show.

As we were climbing out of the car, I saw one of my childhood friends, the now-infamous Gayle King lingering outside with a man named Buddy. He was accompanied by his sister who was dressed in a pants suit with a flower tucked behind her ear. I pretended not to notice the mysterious woman watching me, or the way she and Gayle turned to look in my direction before exchanging a giggle as we approached them. Kevin and I walked up to Gayle to say hi, and then we all walked in together. When we got inside, she introduced me.

"John, this is my boyfriend's sister, Lennice," Gayle said, pushing the girl towards me. Lennice looked up at me with a shy smile. "Hi John," she shouted over the music, holding out her hand. "Hi Lennice," I said, taking her hand in mine and leaning down to speak into her ear. She told me she was impressed with how accurately and easily I'd parked the car. I tried to brush it off as no big deal, but inside I was beaming.

Pretty soon, Kevin and I excused ourselves to the bar to get some drinks. As we did a lap around the small club, I sipped my sloe gin fizz and asked Kevin what I should do about Lennice. I could tell she was into me, and even though by now I'd mostly gotten over my fear of women, I still struggled with knowing how to approach them. I couldn't figure out if I should play it cool, try not to come off as over-eager or just reciprocate her obvious interest. Kevin laughed and told me to just ask her to dance.

We walked back towards the girls who were huddled together in a corner with Buddy, laughing loudly with cups of vodka and orange juice in their hands. I approached Lennice and asked her if she wanted to dance with me, and she smiled widely and nodded yes. At first, I was a little awkward, and I moved as though my shoes were too big for my feet. But Lennice was a natural, and she grabbed my hand to quell my nerves. As it turned out, she was an incredible dancer and we spent the next few hours with our bodies pushed close together, dancing the night away.

Following that night, it became routine for us to meet at Mr. P's. I cherished those evenings we spent together. Our bodies had natural chemistry, and when we were on the dance floor, it was as though we were the only ones there. Eventually, I asked Lennice out on a date and we met up during the daylight hours, far away from that smoky, cramped dance floor.

I knew Lennice really liked me, and I liked her, as well. But at the same time, I was a little confused about what I wanted. I had never been in a real relationship before, and for the first time in my life, girls were starting to pay attention to me. There was a part of me that wanted to linger in that phase, to savor the attention without actually committing to its purveyors. But the more time I spent with Lennice, the more I realized how special she was. I couldn't deny that our chemistry existed beyond the dance floor.

It wasn't long before we were in a full-blown relationship. She introduced me to her family, who were all extremely close, and I began to spend a lot of my free time with them, as well. On the weekends, they'd have a big cookout where we'd hang out, eat food, dance and laugh together. The way they welcomed me into the fold, as though I were one of them, sold me on Lennice even more.

When we first met, Lennice had been working for the State of New Jersey in an administrative role. She'd always loved working with kids and had an interest in nursing. Shortly after we started dating, she decided to enroll in the nursing program at Mercer, a decision I encouraged and supported.

At around the same time, I was finishing up my business administration program, and trying to decide what my next steps would be. I was still in close contact with Ms. Voncile and the two Marthas, and they encouraged me to apply to some universities to further my education. Along with helping me fill out and send applications to several schools, they helped me find and apply to various grants and scholarships so I could offset my tuition. Not long after, the acceptance letters began rolling in. Rutgers

University, Howard University, University of Iowa, Montclair State – I got accepted into more schools than I could keep track of. It was a little bit of an ego boost to realize not only the potential I possessed but that I was a sought-after candidate. I had something all of these schools wanted.

Eventually, I settled on Fairleigh Dickinson University. They had a well-known and well-regarded business management program that really drew me in. Additionally, I had done my research on all of the schools I got into, and one of the things that attracted me to FDU was the fact that it was predominantly white. It might seem like an odd thing to factor into my choice, but hear me out. I had grown up in a mostly Black neighborhood, and I always went to mostly Black schools. I didn't have very much experience being around or working with white people. I knew that eventually when I graduated and entered the workforce, I'd likely be working with many different kinds of people, so I wanted to dip my foot into that pool and acclimate to the differences before I was required to jump in with both feet. For lack of better words, I wanted to see how the other side lived.

In 1981, I graduated from Mercer County Community College and received an Associate Degree in Business Administration. Dad, my sisters, and my best friend Kevin all came to the ceremony, which was held at the Westminster Campus, twenty minutes outside of Trenton. My graduation was a big milestone for my family. For one thing, I was going to continue my education and get my bachelors at FDU. But I was also the first person in my family to ever graduate from college. I had come such a long way from my humble beginnings and mild aspirations.

More importantly, I felt deep in my heart that Mom was looking down on me, and that she was proud of the man I was becoming. It had only been a few short years since she'd died, but I still thought about her nearly every day. And on the day of my graduation from Mercer, I felt her around me, her spirit like a soft wind fanning my graduation gown.

A few short months later, I headed off to FDU to start their business administration program. The school was in Rutherford, about 67 miles away from Trenton, and I moved into the dorms on campus. My roommate was a guy named Greg Foster. I had never lived with a stranger before so at first, it was a struggle having someone else in my space and face all the time, especially in such tight quarters. But soon enough, we got used to each other's presence. We learned to navigate around each other, and how to cope with each other's differences. Greg liked to study with the TV on and music playing, whereas I needed quiet to get anything done. If Greg was studying in the room, I'd go to the library instead. When Greg's mom came to visit him, she'd always bring me an extra slice of crumb cake or her famous giant burgers (she'd caught on to the fact that her son was stingy and didn't like to share). Regardless of his quirks, Greg and I eventually became friends. It probably helped that I wasn't in the room that often, as I was involved in so many different activities on campus.

I played basketball and football, and I was a resident assistant. I also got involved with the Black Student Union, too. I'd first heard about it from Greg, who suggested I run for president. I was hesitant at first; what did I know about leadership or running a full-fledged organization? But Greg was adamant that I would be great at the role and he nominated me for the position. His belief in me was bewildering at first, but it also gave me a sense of confidence. There must have been something in me that inspired that kind of trust, even if I didn't necessarily see it at the time. Others must have agreed because I got the job.

At first, I was deeply uncomfortable. I didn't know how to navigate this new position of authority. I was responsible for so many things and people. I had to address their questions and concerns, and to answer to the folks I was now serving. Thankfully, I didn't have to do it alone. Another student named Bryant was nominated as my Vice President. He was much more familiar with the processes and procedures we had to follow, and he helped me work through everything. In all honesty, Bryant was the brains of the operation, and I was mostly following his lead. He'd come up with ideas, I'd work on their execution, and together, we made an excellent team.

There was also a local pastor, Mr. Frazier, who worked on campus and was in charge of the Education

Opportunity Fund. Mr. Frazier served as an advisor to the BSU, so if I ever encountered any issues I didn't know how to address, he was a helpful source to go to.

Despite the challenges I faced, being President of the Black Student Union was a crash course in leadership and management. I had to learn to balance a budget and allocate the funds allotted to us efficiently. That meant creating consensus within the group for how we wanted to spend the money, as well as what activities and events we wanted to invest in. If there wasn't consensus, it was up to me to navigate those disagreements to a successful outcome. I had to remain open-minded and attentive to the needs of the group, but also assertive and decisive. I won't say I always succeeded at being what I needed to be, but I was open to criticism and if I did mess up, I always tried to stay accountable. That's probably what helped me do as well as I did in the role.

Outside of schoolwork and my extracurriculars, I was still trying to figure out my relationship with Lennice. We were together for most of my time at FDU, but we broke up and got back together often. I loved her, and I knew she loved me, but that wasn't exactly enough to keep us united. We were in a long distance relationship, which obviously complicated things even more. I tried to go home every weekend to spend time with her. And when she graduated from Mercer, I attended her graduation and even stayed with her for a few days to celebrate. But when I became a resident assistant, I had to stay on campus more often, so leaving every weekend to be with my girlfriend was no longer an option; I had responsibilities to attend to. This didn't help our relationship, and for a while, I was unsure if we even had a future together.

However, In 1982, when I just started my final year at FDU, our relationship shifted in a very serious, very consequential way when Lennice became pregnant. When she first told me, I almost doubled over in shock. I could barely muster up a proper sentence, with only stammers of the word 'how?' managing to make its way out my mouth. I wasn't prepared to be a father just yet. I'd barely stepped fully into manhood. But I couldn't straddle the line anymore, making half-baked promises about our future while I chewed on my doubts. I had to fully commit to the relationship, to give her more of myself, and to grow up quickly.

I had no real reason to have doubts about Lennice or our relationship. She loved me, genuinely and sincerely. She saw me and cared for me in a way no other girls had. After she got pregnant, I grew more serious about our relationship and began thinking about the future in a way I hadn't been required to before. I had been looking forward to just exploring things and taking my time, but now, my ending at FDU would coincide with the arrival of my child, and a child who would require a lot of care and resources. I didn't have the privilege of reflection, or embarking on a journey of self-exploration, like so many of my classmates. I had to get real and serious. *Fast*.

In the spring of 1983, I graduated from FDU. This time, Lennice was in attendance, along with our baby who sat heavy and full in her growing round belly. I must have been one of the only students at graduation with a child on the way. While other students were there with their parents, siblings, and friends, I had my own family to be by my side. Dad was there too, with Paulette and Arlene. And Kevin made it out for the ceremony, as well. Even though this was my biggest achievement yet, graduating from university with a Bachelor's Degree in Business Management made the entire event feel heavier than any of my others. Unlike every other graduation I'd had before, the next phase of my life seemed full of possibilities. The world was opening up for me, and this time, there existed something more serious and meaningful than ever before. I was embarking on a whole new journey I didn't feel quite ready for. But as I'd already learned many times before, time waits for no one. Life happens to you, whether you're prepared or not.

A few short months later, in August of 1983, Lennice and I were hanging out together, preparing her house for the baby's arrival, when her water broke. I felt panicked but I tried my best not to let it show. After getting her into the car, we drove over to Mercer Hospital. Lennice had a long, strained birth. Our baby seemed as nervous to enter the world as we were to receive him. After being in labor for nearly the whole day, our son was born that evening.

As soon as I saw him, his little body and his tiny perfect face, I felt something inside of me shift in a way I hadn't anticipated, nor felt before. I was immediately transformed. *I had a son*, *a baby boy*. I thought of my own father, of the monumental role he'd played in my life. Up until that moment, I didn't know what it meant to live for anyone other than myself, to have a purpose that extended beyond my own periphery. But, from the moment our baby entered our lives, and looked up at me with his curious eyes, I barely existed in my own mind anymore. I knew instantly that the rest of my life would be spent building a better world for him, for my son, John Jr.

Chapter 4

Eyes on the Prize

There's nothing in the world that lights a fire under your ass like becoming a father. It transforms your whole perspective on the past, the present, and the future. You see the actions of your own dad a little bit differently (either with more or less compassion, depending on the circumstances). Life becomes tinged with a sense of urgency, pushing you to take action with an intensity unlike anything you've felt before. From the moment your child enters the world, it's as if all of a sudden, you are keenly aware of how much the future depends on you. I didn't quite know who I wanted to be when John Jr. was born, but I knew I had to figure it out, and quickly.

Farleigh, the university I graduated from just a few months before my son was born, had a career center where dozens of companies and employers would seek out ambitious college students and recent graduates to join their teams. Reverend Ray Frazier, who had mentored me while I was president of the Black student union, advised me to pay the center a visit and apply for some of the available positions. He insisted that it was a good way to get my foot in the door.

He wasn't wrong. There were so many companies looking for talent they could hire and train. Airlines, department stores, investment houses, banks – the options were endless. I applied for anything that sounded even remotely interesting, especially companies that offered management training programs. I knew I wanted to do something in business, but the how and what were still unclear. I figured that I'd be okay anywhere I landed, since I was a quick learner and I enjoyed proving myself.

At the time, I was living on the third floor of my sister Paulette's house in Trenton. Lennice and John Jr. were living not too far away, with her family. One day, while I was relaxing on the couch, Paulette knocked on my door before peeking her head inside the room.

"Hey John, you got a phone call," she said, before heading back out again. I figured it was Lennice, and I pushed myself up and ran down the stairs.

"Hello?" I spoke casually into the phone, tucking it between my ear and my shoulder.

"Hi John, this is Diane Tracey from Bowery Savings Bank. How are you doing?" My back stiffened. Bowery Savings Bank was offering a management training program that had piqued my interest more than any of the others. Essentially, it was a year-long program that offered the opportunity to spend some time in every department, learning the ins and outs of what they did. At the end, they'd assign you to a department where you'd start your career, working closely with the head of that particular team. The goal of the program was to prepare college graduates to eventually become bank presidents and c-suite executives. It was one of the most highly coveted programs on offer.

Diane told me she'd be on campus the following week to conduct the preliminary interviews with qualified candidates, and she wanted to meet with me. I was so excited, I could barely muster up a response. I eventually managed to stutter out my thanks and a promise that I'd see her in the coming week for our interview.

When the day of my interview came, I dressed up in my Sunday best and stood in front of the mirror, inspecting my appearance. Several thoughts came to mind. I knew that this interview could influence the trajectory of my life from here on out, and could set me on the path to a very promising career. I just had to get Diane to see that I had what it took, and that amidst hundreds of applicants vying for this opportunity, I was most deserving of the job.

About an hour later, I was sitting in a chair opposite Diane, telling her all about myself. I shared with her stories of my childhood, and how I'd been raised. I told her about my parents and siblings, and the wisdom I acquired from my upbringing. I understood the value of hard work because my family exemplified the utmost dedication in their work. Being a team player was ingrained in me as a child, because within my own household, we all had roles to play, and if one person didn't do their job, it caused disorder and chaos for all of us.

Diane had an easy and calming presence that made it easy for me to talk to her. This was surprising considering her position as the Senior Vice President of Training and Development at Bowery. Even though we'd just met, I felt like she'd taken a liking to me, and that my story had intrigued her in some way. Perhaps to appeal to her banking sentiments, I told Diane to view me as an investment. Of course, there's always risks, but if she gave me a shot to prove how capable I was, it would pay off for everyone.

Something I said must have struck a chord. At the end of the interview, Diane invited me to New York for the next stage of the interview process. I was so happy, I couldn't wait to share the good news with Lennice. However, she didn't seem as thrilled about it as I was.

"But if you get the job, then you'll have to move to New York, right?" she asked me, fidgeting nervously. I felt a sting of hurt. I hadn't gotten the job yet, but even getting this far in the interview process was a big accomplishment. I'd hoped she'd be more happy for me. "Well, I gotta get the job first, Lennice," I said, laughing. I tried to keep the energy light and positive, and to reassure her that nothing would change between us. "And if I do, I won't move to New York, I'll just commute there every day for work." She looked at me with her mouth turned downward, but she didn't say anything further. I could tell she wasn't too thrilled by the idea, but that didn't sway me in the least. This was an opportunity of a lifetime, and if I got it, I'd be able to provide for Lennice and John Jr., to give them the life I knew they deserved.

A few weeks later, I boarded the train to New York for my interview. When I arrived, the room was full of 150 eager candidates. The room seethed subtly with an air of competition. I walked in, ready to make myself known, and to fight for my spot. But also immediately, I felt like the odd man out. For one, I was the only Black person in the room, which made me stand out. It was a little strange for me to be in an environment like that, since I'd grown up in majority-Black neighborhoods and went to majority-Black schools, with Fairleigh Dickinson being the exception. I was also wearing a tan suit with a freshly shaped afro. In a sea of gray and blue suits with perfectly coiffed hair, you could pick me out easily.

As everyone else networked, conversing softly with each other while sussing out the competition, I paced alone in a corner trying to center myself. I needed to be clear on my purpose. Why was I there? I gave myself a little pep talk while others around me boasted about their accomplishments, the impressive things they'd already done, and the Ivy League schools they'd attended.

"You're from North Trenton, don't forget where you're from. You deserve this shot. You deserve a seat at this table." I said to myself, pacing nervously back and forth. "Don't forget who you're doing this for, John."

I saw Lennice and John Jr. clearly in my mind. I saw the future that would become accessible to us, to my family, if I pulled this off. I wanted the job badly. And I really felt like I was the perfect guy to do it. It felt like all of the things I'd gone through in life had led me to this point. I may not have gone to Harvard or Columbia, like some of the other candidates, but that didn't make me any less deserving.

A little while later, as I sat there dreaming, praying, and preparing, my name was called. I stood up, smoothed down my jacket, took a deep breath, and walked into the interview room. There was a woman waiting for me. Her name was Grace Pichardo, the Vice President of Training and Development, one position below Diane. Like Diane, I also found her easy to talk to, and I felt like I breezed right through our conversation. But just when I began to get a little comfortable, she dropped a bombshell on me – I still had five more interviews to go. Since whoever got the job would be working with the heads of all departments at the bank, from the commissary all the way up to the chairman's office, they all wanted the opportunity to meet and feel out each candidate.

I gulped down hard, swallowing the nervous ball that had formed at the back of my throat. I thought I'd done a great job with Grace, but could I replicate that success five more times? I didn't have much time to linger on it. After each interview, I only had enough time to straighten up my tie, take a few deep breaths, and try to mentally reset before I had to go back in and do the whole thing all over again. Only this time, with a new cast of judges waiting to dissect my every word.

By the time the interviews were all finished, it was dark outside. I grabbed my coat and dragged myself to Penn Station to make the long commute home. On the walk over, despite my low energy levels, I felt a surge of desire run through me, like lightning in my veins. *I really, really want this job,* I thought to myself. They'd made me fight for it, that much was for sure.

Regardless of the outcome, I felt proud of how well I'd done. I'd made it through the day, and I walked away feeling as though I'd represented myself honestly, and with integrity. Now, all I wanted to do was go home, and straight to bed.

Later that evening, after I finally made it home, I got a phone call. I listened as they described how much everyone had liked me, and how I'd impressed them with my charisma and enthusiasm. I stood there, phone in hand, and waited for the ball to drop. For them to tell me that despite all of that, they'd decided to go one with one of the other more experienced, well-connected candidates instead.

Much to my surprise (and delight), they told me I was one of the 12 people they'd picked to enter the program. *I got the job!* I was so excited, I could barely sleep that night. It's strange to say, but I felt like my life was about to change, and pivot in a direction that I'd never even imagined possible before.

I couldn't wait to tell Lennice. I knew she hadn't been that encouraged about it before the interview, but this was such a transformational opportunity for our family. I thought she'd change her tune when she realized that I was picked out of a pool of over 150 candidates, how this job would help to fast track my career, to develop professionally, and, mostly, help us set the foundation for a bright future together. But when I told her, she just stared at me with a look of disappointment on her face that crushed any hope I had in getting her support.

"Why couldn't you find something more local?" she asked, shifting John Jr. from one hip to the other. "There are plenty of banks here in Trenton, John." I exhaled loudly, sighing out a hot breath of frustration. I knew she felt the job would take me away from her and John Jr., and that being in New York would form a wedge between us, forcing us farther and farther apart.

"You should be happy for me, Lennice," I said, rubbing my temples. "You should be happy for our family." I wanted her to realize that my decision to take the job wasn't a selfish one; I was doing it for all of us, for our future. The conversation didn't go well, neither of us willing to budge, both of us feeling hurt and neglected. It was clear that we weren't going to come to a consensus, at least not then, so I dropped it, and spent the next few weeks preparing for the program to begin.

When I finally started working, it was a big departure from how I'd been living my life thus far. I had to be up before the sun every morning to catch the 6 a.m. train to New York. And the job itself was a major crash course on the bank, but on life, too. Every department I trained in, and (almost) every department head I shadowed, taught me invaluable lessons about how to be a better employee, leader, and man, in general.

I started off in the commissary, where I worked with an older woman named Mae. There, I helped prepare food for the workers, cleaned up after meals, and completed other small tasks. Mae acted like a surrogate grandmother, always saving me a big piece of the dessert she made, or heaping an extra scoop of icecream on my plate after lunch. The folks I worked with in the commissary reminded me of the people I grew up around and became a subtle reminder of where I'd come from.

After that, I moved onto accounting. My boss there was a man named Bernie Cannon, an energizing and hard working force of nature. When I arrived in accounting, the bank had just purchased a set of loans from another bank. Our task was to meticulously comb through the documents to ensure the loans and the purchase agreements were all up to Bowery's standards. In accounting, I often worked longer hours than usual, spending nights with my head hunched over a file. Bernie taught me a lot about the importance of having an iron-clad work ethic, and how satisfying it can be to set regular, weekly goals to achieve. This required setting an agenda on Monday, organizing your time in a way that made your goals possible, then dedicating yourself to completing the work to ensure a successful finish by week's end.

The marketing department, which came next, was one of my favorites. Diane was the head of that department. I learned how a marketing campaign went from the ideation stage, to development, and finally to execution. It was fascinating to watch the creative process in action, to see how they took raw data and information from surveys and turned it into art. I also got to watch the team shoot commercials for the bank. At the time, Joe DiMaggio, a New York Yankees legend, was the bank's spokesperson so I got to meet him and see him in action.

When it was Diane's turn to get in front of the camera, she was a wonder to witness. She'd read one line, catch herself, and insist on doing it again and again until she thought it was perfect. To me, every time she did it, it looked as good as the time before. But the more I watched, observing closely, the more I caught the subtle differences – and what a huge difference they made. Diane was an absolute perfectionist, and it showed in the quality of the work she produced. It wasn't good enough to complete a project well, especially if it had the potential to be great.

Next up, I went to the Securities Investment Unit. The woman who headed that team was around the same age as me or just a few years older. In comparison to everyone else in similar positions, she was extremely young. While she did great work, and was a very quick thinker, she seemed unable or perhaps unwilling to answer the many questions I had. Securities is an important department because it was where they invested money for the bank. I often found myself confused and scratching my head, forced to figure things out on my own because I wasn't getting any answers I needed from her. At one point, she went on vacation and I had to do certain tasks in her absence. I had to learn on my feet, sometimes by simply observing and putting the disparate information together myself. It wasn't a perfect system, but I got through that department without causing any damage, so I'd call that a success.

Another important aspect of this year-long program was the relationship we built with our advisor. Each person was paired with a senior member of the bank who we met with at the end of each week to discuss our experiences, ideas, suggestions, or to ask any lingering questions. My advisor was a man named Al Cohen. Al was the executive vice president of the company, and the third man in charge. Out of all the advisors, Al was the most senior, and the company's decision to match me with him felt deliberate. Al was very protective, constantly checking in to make sure I felt comfortable at the company, and that I wasn't running into any issues with other department heads, or being left out of important conversations and meetings. I began to wonder if they'd paired me with him because I was Black. Perhaps having a senior advisor was a means to protect me from potential abuse from other co-workers. If they messed with me, they'd have to deal with Al. And if you knew what was good for you, you didn't mess with Al.

Nonetheless, I loved having Al as my advisor. My desk was in his office, so whenever he had a meeting, he'd call me over to sit in. I'd drag my chair across the room and sit quietly with a pen and notepad, jotting down anything I thought was important or that I wanted to learn more about. At the end of the meeting, Al would let me lob all of my questions at him, answering them with clarity and patience. The opportunities he gave me were priceless; I was learning firsthand from one of the top executives at the bank about how to run a company.

In addition to his generosity with information, Al was also deeply empathetic. After a few months of working at the bank, I'd noticed the gulf in differences between how I dressed compared to the other employees. It wasn't that I didn't dress well, per se, but I felt the same way I did when I showed up to my interview in a tan suit, while everyone else wore more refined colors, like gray and blue. I stuck out. One day, I finally mustered up the courage to approach Al and ask him a question I'd been bouncing around in my head for weeks.

"Mr. Cohen, I know I just started here not that long ago," I stuttered, trying to remember to look him in his face and not at the ground, "but I was wondering if it's possible for me to get a loan from the bank. I think it's important that I upgrade my wardrobe." Al smiled and patted me on the back. Within a few days, I had the money in my hand, and I headed straight to a suit store down the street from the office.

I bought a few suits in just the right colors (leaving the tan ones aside for now), new leather shoes, and some crisp ties in different shades of gray, blue and red. I felt different when I showed up to work in those suits, more professional, and more prepared to take on any task that was thrown at me. I guess it's true what they say; look good, feel even better.

Besides all of the invaluable lessons I was learning from Al, the other department heads, and the bank, in general, Bowery was exposing me to the idea of living a more refined life of luxury. The first flight I ever took was on a business trip with Bowery, when I flew with the Chairman to La Jolla, California. *And it was a first class flight*. The company had given me a stack of money to spend on any expenses I had on the trip. Since the hotel and flight were already paid for, I expected the money to just go to food. But the Chairman ended up taking me to a restaurant his son owned in La Jolla, all expenses paid. When we sat down at the table, the servers set a 4 lb lobster out in front of me. Now, I'd never had lobster in my life, and I didn't even know how to go about eating that thing. But someone came back and cracked it open, exposing a heap of steaming, buttery meat. After dinner, they brought out a slice of chocolate cake that was nearly as big as my head. At the end, I tried to give back the money left over from the expenses to the Chairman. He just laughed and shook his head.

"No John, keep it." I'd never been exposed to these kinds of extravagances before. Not until I started working at Bowery. I was getting a front row view into how the 'other side' lived, and it was then that I realized what I'd been missing. I remember one time, I was on a business trip to West Sulphur Springs, West Virginia. They had booked us rooms at the Greenbrier, which just so happened to be a former slave plantation, a fact that didn't sit well with me. The hotel was set on a massive, 11,000 acre property, surrounded by endless woods. They'd preserved the historic feel of the building, which felt oddly unsettling. After dinner, I headed up to my room to go to bed. When I got there, I noticed that my bed linen had been turned down, as if ready for someone to get into bed, and there were chocolates on my pillow. Alarmed, I called down to the concierge to report that someone had been in my room – and strangely, they'd left their dessert behind.

The woman proceeded to explain the concept of 'turn down service' to me, something I had no idea existed before that day. It seemed like such a strange concept, but I suppose it was a luxury you got used to when you had money to burn.

Bowery was changing my life in ways I hadn't anticipated at all. Another thing I hadn't expected was for Lennice to be so right about what might happen to our relationship after I got the job. I usually left the house before dawn for work, and didn't get home until 7:30 p.m., or sometimes even later. This left very little time for me to spend with her and John Jr. Our relationship turned rocky, and we'd break up and get back together often, seemingly unsure of how we were meant to fit into each other's lives. I knew I loved Lennice, and I loved that we already had a family together. But things were becoming too difficult and at times, breaking up felt like the more convenient, peaceful solution to our relationship woes. Nonetheless, we worked at it the best we could. Suffice to say, work was my number one priority at this time. I was trying to establish myself, and to turn my career into something with the potential to support my family for the rest of our lives.

In 1984, after finishing my tour of the different departments, I was assigned to work in Appraisals, under a man named Vinnie Palladino. Vinnie was a thoughtful leader, and he taught me a lot when I worked under him. Being in appraisals also exposed me to the world of real estate. There, we had the task of inspecting and valuing homes – brownstones, family homes, co-ops, condominiums, you name it. That exposure naturally lent it itself to a deeper understanding of the home buying process, which I quickly realized was a lot easier than I'd expected. The longer I spent in appraisals, the more I found myself itching to buy a home of my own. I'd been living with my sister for nearly two years, but I had a son and sometimes girlfriend (we were broken up at this time) to take care of.

I started researching the housing market in Trenton, seeing what kind of houses were available, and at what price. As it turned out, they were even more affordable than I'd hoped. One day, while on my search, I found an advertisement for a special program in New Jersey sponsored by National State Bank that offered low interest rates for first-time homebuyers. The flier indicated that if you were someone looking to buy your first house, applications started at 9:00 a.m., the following Monday. I didn't want to miss out on the chance, and for whatever reason, I believed that by Monday morning there would be a line out the door. Without consulting Lennice, or anyone else, I drove up to Perth Amboy, New Jersey, Sunday night. When I got there, I took out the lawn chair and blanket I'd packed, and camped out right outside the bank's front door. As it turned out, I wasn't the only one with that idea. A few others showed up after me, setting up their makeshift beds to wait till morning. At 9:00 a.m., I was the first one in the office.

After I filled out my application, I spoke with the Chairman and told him that I was applying for a loan at National State Bank, and asked if he could put in a good word for me. He agreed, and he sent a letter to the president. Within no time, I got the mortgage.

The fun part was finding a house. I didn't mind something that needed work, as I enjoyed fixing things and working with my hands. I knew I wanted something big enough to accommodate a family, and located in a decent neighborhood. Before long, I found the perfect spot. It was more of a fixer upper than I'd initially wanted, but it was a large and beautiful home with solid bones. Plus, the neighborhood was spectacular. I figured it would take me a while to fix it, since I could only put in time on the weekends and during the summer. But it was a labor of love. I poured everything into that house, spending every weekend repairing floors, installing tiles and carpeting, removing walls, and figuring out the plumbing and electrical wiring. I was in no rush to move in, so I didn't really mind.

Around this same time, I forged a strong connection with the senior vice president of the residential division, a man named Pazel Jackson, who also happened to be one of the only Black executives at Bowery.

Pazel was a consummate professional, always decked out in a bow or straight tie and a crisp, elegant suit. He had a presence and an air about him that commanded attention, but also respect. He is, till this day, one of the most articulate men I've ever met. He had such a powerful way with words, and could string them together to sell nearly anything.

Pazel became a mentor to me, guiding me through both life and my career. He helped me maneuver difficult situations, and gave me advice when I didn't know what to do. I think he saw something in me that he wanted to nurture. He told me about opportunities he believed I was well-suited for and avenues to pursue to further my career in an upward trajectory.

After working in appraisals for about a year, I moved into residential lending. Pazel thought I'd benefit from taking part in a special credit training program for commercial lending, so I could expand my expertise beyond the residential realm. He recommended me for it, but in the end, Pazel's superior, the executive vice president, Conrad Stevenson, decided not to approve my application.

Pazel was vexed about the rejection, but I decided to just move forward anyway. Pazel ended up moving to another bank shortly after. For the next year, I became something of an expert at residential lending, and eventually they gave me the responsibility of overseeing the whole department. I took the expanded responsibilities with enthusiasm, as I saw the potential behind putting in all the hard work needed to make myself indispensable to the company. By 1986, the CEO of Bowery, a man named Dick Ravitch, assigned me to a special project. I was tasked with going out and purchasing $50 million worth of loans. Over the next few weeks, I worked with various investment banking institutions in the city, putting together a portfolio for Dick to approve.

While I was busy working on Dick's request, the newly hired Executive Vice President and COO, Ed Grebow, had been going from department to department, putting immense pressure on the team to reduce their expenses. I didn't have any personal interactions with the guy, thankfully, but from what I'd heard, he was doing his best to put the fear of God into the staff. If they didn't get expenses down, he promised them there would be hell to pay.

By the time I'd finalized the portfolio and got it into Dick's hands, he had a whole new host of requests. He wanted more of one type of loan, and less of another. I felt overwhelmed, but determined to get him what he needed. I felt as though my performance in completing this task would either make or break me, in his eyes. It could set me up for even more opportunities, or, on the flipside, if he didn't get what he wanted, he could take future opportunities away. I left his office that afternoon with a feeling of urgency in the pit of my stomach, but also with a renewed sense of purpose. I was going to get it right. I had to.

Well, that's what I thought. The next day, it was announced that Bowery Savings Bank had been sold. I felt blindsided; I hadn't seen it coming at all. Here I was, working my ass off to get this 'special assignment' fulfilled for Dick, while he and Ed were plotting their plan the whole time. It felt crushing at first, because I really had banked so much of my future in Bowery. Even though I'd only been there for a few years, I'd managed to steadily work my way up, and I believed I had a position as a future executive in the company. After all, I'd come to Bowery from the management training program with the expectation that eventually, I might become the bank's president. I was ambitious, but with good reason. Now, I felt as though those dreams had been buried alive.

I didn't feel too bad for too long though. Pazel Jackson, who'd mentored me for years at Bowery, reached out to me shortly after the news was announced. He'd moved over to Chemical Bank a little over a year earlier, and had established himself there. Chemical Bank, unlike Bowery, was a commercial lending institution. They weren't really in the business of residential loans – though they had been wanting to expand into it. Luckily, I had just the right experience to bring to the table. Pazel told me that Chemical wanted me to do for them what I had done for Bowery. In other words, if I wanted the job, it was mine for the taking. So, shortly after leaving Bowery, I began my new job at Chemical Bank. 1986 was shaping up to be an exciting year for me, one of big changes and deliberate movement. And it was only getting started.

That spring, Lennice and I had broken up and started seeing other people. We remained friends, and she'd often come by the new house and help me clean. We still had a child together, and realistically I'd purchased the house for him to live in. But things between us had just been rocky for so long that a split was imminent.

By the time summer rolled around, I was crushing hard on a young woman named Monica. I'd always had a thing for her, and now that I was single, I figured it was time for me to shoot my shot. I invited her to come by my house to check it out and see the progress I'd made. She said she'd like that, so I gave her the address.

A few days later, Lennice was over at the house with me, helping me tidy up the yard. Inconveniently, that's exactly when Monica decided to drop by. Even though Lennice and I weren't together, it still created an awkward dynamic, so as the two women sat together, I excused myself to do something else.

Despite my age, I still hadn't quite mastered the art of pursuing women. As Monica and Lennice chatted away, I tried to think of how to let Monica know I wanted to give a relationship with her a shot. Little did I know, Lennice was having her own conversation with

Monica in the yard. She left shortly after, a cold air trailing behind her. Lennice, for her part, was perfectly content, raking the dead grass with a smile on her face.

A few days later, Monica called me and asked me a very pointed question: what are you trying to do here? I was confused, and asked her what she meant.

"Are you trying to talk to me, or are you getting back with Lennice? Which one is it?" I was stunned. Lennice and I hadn't even talked about getting back together, so I was baffled at where she'd heard this. At first, I thought it might be because Lennice had been at the house. But we had a child together, that was a perfectly reasonable explanation that a smart woman like Monica must have considered.

"What do you mean, Monica?" I asked, my voice low. "Where did you hear that?"

"Lennice told me, John. She told me everything."

Suddenly, it all made sense. Monica's icy departure from my house, and Lennice's light and happy energy. I couldn't help but to laugh. I hadn't expected Lennice to try to sabotage a potential relationship with someone I really liked. But for some reason, I wasn't upset. In fact, I felt something else: love.

When I finally confronted Lennice about it, she owned up to everything, admitting that she'd told Monica we were getting back together. I began to see her in a new light. It was as if I'd been blind for so long, always looking around for the next best thing. But the entire time I failed to realize that the most I could ever want was standing right in front of me, waiting to be seen. I felt a sting of guilt, like perhaps I hadn't appreciated or noticed everything Lennice had done and been for me. But I was determined to make things right.

Later that week, I went to a jewelry store on my lunch break from work. As I hovered over the counter, staring down at the shimmering bands below, a sales agent came over to help. He asked me what my budget was and then pulled out all of the different options within my range. As soon as I saw the ring, I knew it was the one. It had a silver band and a round, glimmering white diamond. It was classic and elegant – all things that reminded me so much of Lennice.

"I'll take it," I told the agent.

When I was back at work, I called Lennice and told her to come by the house later on and she agreed. In the evening, I heard her car pull into the driveway and I took in a large gulp of air, trying to steady myself. I fiddled with the little black box in my pocket, going over what I was going to say in my head. But as soon as she walked into the house, my planned speech seemed to melt into a distant place in my brain, one that wasn't immediately accessible to me.

I gave her a hug, and stared down at her for a second before telling her what was on my mind. I told her that I'd realized that she was the one for me, that she was the only person I wanted to kiss or ever wanted to love. I knew she loved me, and no other woman had made me feel as wanted and desired as she had.

At this point, I got down on one knee, pulled the box out of my pocket and opened it, holding it up to the woman I hoped would become my future wife.

"Lennice, I want to be with you forever, to continue building our family, and our life together. Will you marry me?"

She gasped. I don't think a proposal was at all what she'd expected when I asked her to come over that night. She stared down at me, her eyes wide, as if waiting for me to change my mind. And then, after a few seconds had passed, she squealed with delight, held out her hand and shouted, 'yes, of course!'

I placed the ring on her finger and stood to kiss her, to hold her in my arms. We stood that way for a few minutes, and then I told Lennice that I had a few conditions. If we were doing this, I wanted to do it soon – before the end of the year (which, as it happened, was only three short months away).

My proposal and our engagement came as a shock to many people. Almost everyone, other than the few coworkers I'd confided in, thought Lennice and I were still broken up. Still, our family and friends quickly got into the spirit of helping us plan a Christmas-themed wedding.

The next three months passed by in a blur of invitations, colored ribbon, wedding dress shopping, cake tasting, and pre-wedding jitters. Our wedding date was December 27, 1986. On the morning of the big day, I woke up feeling energized and a little nervous. I'd thought about this day for years, even before I'd met Lennice. I always wondered how I'd feel, what thoughts would be going through my head. Now that it was here, I found myself thinking about my mother.

In a way, I'd dreaded my wedding day for so long simply because I knew Mom wouldn't be there. I didn't feel dread though, as I'd expected. Instead, I felt sad, and I missed her dearly. But I also felt like she would have been happy with my choice, that she would have welcomed Lennice into our family with her big, glowing smile, and warm embrace. I felt her presence around me, and it gave me comfort; something I desperately needed for the long day to come.

We had a large wedding, with close to 350 people in attendance. Our wedding theme was red and white, so I was decked out in a suit that adorned both colors. When our ceremony began, everything seemed to be going as planned. After Lennice's father walked her down the aisle, we both stood together, side by side, facing the pastor, ready for him to marry us. Behind him, my friend Reverend Joe Leonard was on the piano, where just minutes before, he'd performed.

Before the pastor could begin the ceremony, Joe broke out into song, singing *'there's nothing but love for the two of you,'* much to the surprise of the entire congregation, including us. The pastor turned his head, clearly taken aback by the outburst. Joe wasn't the greatest singer in the world, but he sang with heart and soul.

When he finished, everything else went on without a hitch. The wedding was perfect. More than anything, I was excited to be starting our life together – Lennice, John Jr., and me. It was impossible not to feel as though my life was on its way up, like I was flying high.

I had a beautiful wife. My son was almost four years old. We had a big house, one that I'd nearly built with my own hands. I had a job that I loved, and felt valued at. Life was good. I had no idea what else life had in store for me, but I was excited to find out.

Chapter 5

Sink or Swim

There are times when I look back at my life, and I feel like I went to sleep one night as a boy, and woke up the next morning a man, along with all its pressures and responsibilities. The first few years after Lennice and I got married were a crash course on the true meaning of duty and obligation. Even though we'd been a couple for years and had a son, we'd never lived together. We co-parented John Jr., but since it was always done in our own respective homes, it never felt like we were actually doing it together. Once we moved into the house that I'd poured so much of my time and energy into, we finally felt like a family.

It was a beautiful thing to leave for work every morning knowing that I had a wife and son to come back to. With that also came the weight of knowing I needed to take care of them, and to ensure I was fulfilling my role as the protector and provider of my family. But I liked having people depend on me; to have a defined purpose in my life. It filled me with pride to know that everything I did and built was for them. They were the beneficiaries of all of my hard work. And within no time, our family grew even bigger.

In 1988, Lennice gave birth to our second son, Joshua. In a strange way, I felt my heart broadening, growing more spacious to accommodate the unfathomable amount of love I was carrying. One night, a few months after his birth, we were laying in bed together with Josh sleeping between us. I stared down at him, his chest rising and falling softly, and I felt a surge of overwhelming pride and adoration.

"I want five of them," I said, not moving my gaze from Josh's face.

"Five of what?" Lennice asked, propping herself up on her elbow, caressing Josh's cheek.

"I want five boys. John and Josh should grow up surrounded by brothers, just like I did." Lennice laughed, shaking her head.

"Five?! We'll see about that, John," she chuckled, a soft, content smile etched on her face. "Let's focus on these guys first." We interlocked our fingers, and I kissed her hand. Little did we both know, our third child was coming sooner than we'd anticipated. We found out Lennice was pregnant again just a few months later.

With another baby on the way, Lennice and I decided we needed an even bigger house, something that could accommodate our growing family. It hadn't necessarily been in our plan to move, but we had to do what was best for the kids. We found a beautiful 4-bedroom home in Ewing, a town just five miles from Trenton. It was also in a better neighborhood than the one we lived in, with access to excellent schools for the kids.

Just a few short months after we'd moved into our new house and gotten settled in, Lennice's sister came to stay with us for a few days. Lennice was 9 months pregnant and had been having a particularly rough time. One night, after dinner, she began feeling sick, with small quakes of pain ripping through her stomach. We figured she'd probably be giving birth soon, but since her water hadn't broken yet, we thought we had time.

A few hours of gradually escalating pain later, it became clear that we had to get Lennice to the hospital fast. But she was in so much pain, it took forever to even get out the door. After getting her into the passenger seat of the car, with her legs stretched out in front of her, I rushed towards the hospital. We barely made it a block away before Lennice began screaming.

"He's coming John, he's coming! I can't wait!" her voice was laced with pain and urgency. I pulled over to the side of the road, and before I even had a chance to put the car in park, I heard our son's cry echo throughout the car. When I opened the door, there he was, in a pool of blood between Lennice's legs. I picked him up gently, and with my hands shaking, I placed him on her chest.

I hadn't anticipated this at all. As soon as I made sure they were both safe, I got back into the car and raced towards the hospital, which was in Princeton, about 10 miles away. But as soon as I got onto the highway, I saw red and blue lights flashing in my rear-view.

"I can't believe this," I said to myself, my heart bursting through my chest. As soon as the officer came to my window, I told him what had happened.

"Officer, I know I was going fast. But my wife just gave birth. We need to get to the hospital. Right now," I said quickly, my words blurring together as I gestured beside me. The cop peered into the window, and his face went white. He nodded, then told me he'd drive in front of us with the sirens on.

We arrived at the hospital a few minutes later with our police escorts in tow. As soon as I pulled up, two nurses ran out with a wheelchair. They opened the passenger seat door, ready to pull out a pregnant mom, but instead, they discovered our baby, lying on Lennice's chest, both of them soaked in various bodily fluids. The shock was audible.

"Not what you were expecting, huh?" I snickered, unable to help myself. They helped her out of the car and wheeled the two of them inside while I went to park. I looked into the passenger seat, trying to process what had just happened. *My wife had given birth to our son in the car.* The whole night felt like a scene out of a movie.

"Well, thank God for leather seats," I said, laughing as I rested my head on the steering wheel. The reality of my life began to hit me. I hadn't even broken 30 yet, and I was already a father of three. I shook my head and swallowed hard. I got out of the car and jogged to the front doors of the hospital, excited to meet my son who'd apparently been in a rush to come into the world. After getting to Lennice's room, I was grateful to discover that everyone was doing alright, mother and baby both healthy and resting.

We named our boy Justin. After taking him home the next day, we began to settle into the new flow of our life. Unlike Lennice, who was a pediatric nurse and had a knack for kids, I felt a little shakier with the boys when they were babies. They were so small and fragile, and I was always worried I might accidentally hurt them. But that didn't seem to be much of an issue since I was away at work most of the time anyway. Since my job at Chemical Bank was based in New York, I usually left home at the crack of dawn to start my commute to the city, and didn't make it home until late in the evening, just in time for dinner. I'd try to spend as much time with the boys as I could, to give them my full attention. But in all honesty, Lennice did most of the work in keeping the boys alive and happy around this time.

Pretty soon, work got even more intense. One day, not long after Justin's birth, my boss pulled me into his office and informed me that I was being relocated to Long Island. The company made it clear that they'd do whatever it took to get me there, including taking care of the move and getting my family set up in a new home. I felt torn. On the one hand, I was happy to discover how valued and indispensable I'd become to the company. It was clear that I'd made an impact. But on the other hand, I had no desire to move to Long Island. In fact, it was out of the question. Lennice and I had just moved the kids into a new home in Ewing, and we'd barely been there for a year.

I shared my concerns with my superiors and we were able to come to a compromise. They understood that I was unwilling to move to Long Island, but the commute there wasn't so much longer than New York.

"Get there when you get there, leave when you need to leave," they instructed me. The point was abundantly clear; they *needed* me. While it felt great to be needed, I also felt a pull of obligation. Chemical Bank had picked me up after I left Bowery. I especially felt a sense of loyalty to Pazel Jackson. He recognized my value at a pivotal moment in my life, and transformed my misfortune into an opportunity to make an even bigger mark. It helped that I happened to love my job, too.

I agreed to the transfer, and began commuting to Long Island. I still left the house early in the morning, but now I was getting home nearly an hour later every night. I didn't mind so much at first, but after a few months, the extra time commuting began to wear me down. By the time I got home, I was too tired to spend any time with Lennice and the boys. My work had taken over my entire life, and had left us with minimal moments to enjoy to experience as a family.

I spoke with my bosses and told them that I couldn't do it anymore. It had become unsustainable. They told me they understood, but they were sad to see me go. They offered me a severance package of six months pay plus benefits. When I got home later that night and told Lennice that I'd quit my job, she was understandably upset. Our family depended on my paychecks, on my ability to keep a roof over our heads and put food on the table. But now, I was unemployed for the first time since I was a boy.

It was a strange feeling that was both liberating and suffocating at the same time. I had so much freedom to explore what direction I wanted to venture out into next. But I also recognized the reality that my sons' future depended on whichever path I chose. It was my job to provide for my family, a truth hardwired into my brain.

Since working at the bank, and especially within residential lending, I'd become interested in real estate. I'd toyed with the idea of getting licensed before, but had never pulled the trigger, as I'd been preoccupied with my day job. Now, that desire came rushing back.

I enrolled in the Weichert Real Estate School and completed the course a few weeks later. After that, I sat for the exam, which I passed with ease. Within a month of starting, I was a licensed real estate agent. But as soon as I finished, I found myself at a loss for what to do with it. It dawned on me that I'd have to work for an agency for a while, at least until I established myself, which meant working for commission. I was unsettled by the thought of having my livelihood hinge on something so precarious, especially at such a slippery time for the economy. The country was in a recession and housing sales were not doing so hot.

I felt lost and unsure of myself, and I didn't even have a job to distract me. One evening, I was sitting with my older brother Eddie, and I shared with him my predicament. He was also unemployed at the time, so he could empathize with what I was going through. He was in the trucking industry, and even though he wasn't working at the time, he knew there were ample opportunities to make a lot of money. Many shipping companies would hire truck owners to transport goods using their vehicles. According to him, there was a lot of money to be made. Interestingly enough, I always thought that I'd end up working with cars and trucks, since that was where my first passion was born, but especially because it was what I'd grown up within, and around. My dad drove and worked in trucks, as did my brother, my uncle and other family members. After talking to Eddie, my interest was piqued. Coincidentally the more I mulled it over, the more it seemed like the opportunities were looking for me, too. I came across a few ads for a company called Truck Way, looking for truck owners and operators to assist with shipments. I called them, and inquired about how their operations worked, and what one could expect to be paid.

As they explained, Truck Way supplied everything except for the truck. If there was a shipment to be delivered, the driver would be dispatched. They'd hitch the Truck Way trailer to their truck, transport the goods and then get paid shortly after. All the driver had to do was show up with their vehicle when called and drive; Truck Way did everything else. I called my dad, who was living in Virginia at the time, and asked him for some advice. He told me he thought it sounded like a good opportunity, and encouraged me to give it a shot. Buoyed by his support, I spoke with Eddie, who was already a licensed truck driver. We spoke about the possibility of us starting something together, and I told him that I was considering buying a truck. I asked him if he would be interested in working for me. It would resolve both of our unemployment issues, while presenting an opportunity for substantial financial gain. He was excited about the possibility, which only furthered my own determination. He was okay with being my employee, which was an important relationship dynamic I wanted to establish right from the jump.

I spoke with Lennice about my idea, though by this point I'd already made up my mind. She wasn't too keen on my plan. Understandably, she would have much preferred that I just return to the bank, and to the safety and security of a steady paycheck, *with* benefits. But she told me that if I wanted to give it a shot, she'd stand by me. I'd hoped she'd be more enthusiastic about the new venture, but I understood her perspective. Entrepreneurship is risky, and we had a family to provide for, which meant many hungry mouths to feed. But I had a good feeling about it. Plus, we still had the severance checks coming in like clockwork. Whatever I made with the trucking enterprise would be a supplement to my current income. In Lennice's mind, if I hadn't secured a steady income by the time the severance payments stopped coming, I'd just return to the bank. But I didn't let myself go there. I was confident the trucking business would work out.

My first order of business was to buy a truck. I searched the newspapers and eventually found a used one that I paid for with cash. Within no time at all, Eddie and I were out on the road. Since he was the driver, I would accompany him on trips, learning the order of the road. Even though I was technically the boss, I was also his student in this scenario. Sure, I'd grown up around trucks, but since then, I'd become more of a white-collar worker. I wore suits and worked in an office, but this was Eddie's life. As a truck driver with years of experience, he taught me the ropes, and showed me in real time how to drive the truck, to load the shipments, and how to hitch the trailer. After a few months of watching him, I got my trucking license, too.

As I gained more and more knowledge on the technical side of the business, the money steadily began to flow in. Working with Truck Way took most of the thinking out of the job, since we didn't have to do the work to secure clients. We worked, in a way, like a delivery service, like Uber for large transports.

Within three months, we were doing exceptionally well. So well, in fact, Eddie suggested I get another truck for myself. His proposition was partially the result of being sick of me riding along with him every day, but it wasn't a bad idea. If I bought another truck, we could bring in double our profit. After purchasing a second used truck, we were raking in an impressive amount of money. But instead of making me comfortable, it made me curious. If we were making that much cash, Truck Way was indubitably bringing in much, much more. They took a sizable chunk out of every contract we fulfilled, even though we were doing most of the labor. Working for them took the guesswork out of our job, yes, but it also left a lot of money on the table – money I would've preferred stayed in my pocket.

Power Moves

As is often the case with me, as soon as the idea entered my mind, I couldn't shake it off. If I got the authority from the Interstate Commercial Courier (ICC) on my own, then I could book loads directly with corporations, versus working through a third party. My costs would go up, as I'd have to buy more trucks and some trailers, too, and I'd also have to pay for the insurance. But, on the upside, I'd be making significantly more money. I'd be able to hire other owner-operators, like Eddie and I, which, in turn, would increase our workload.

Before I even had time to fully think things through, an opportunity presented itself. There was a trucking company I knew of that was downsizing, which meant they were getting rid of some of their equipment. They offered me two trucks and two trailers for no money down – all I had to do was take over the payments. This would alleviate one of my biggest concerns; how to get the capital for downpayments on equipment? By acquiring their equipment, it would save the business from drying out our cash flow. It seemed like too good of a deal to pass up, so I agreed.

Just like that, Harmon Transfer Corp., my fourth baby, was born. Now, I had four trucks, two trailers, and the freedom to identify opportunities and book direct freights myself. Since my dad had worked in the industry for so long, he had many deeply established connections, which Eddie and I were able to leverage to secure more contracts, and hire even more drivers.

The trucking industry is heavily dependent on networking and forging strong relationships. That meant, if you do well with a client or contract, it had the ability to snowball into many more, simply through referrals. I tried not to get overly excited about how quickly the business was growing, but I felt good, like the stars were aligning in my favor. Business was booming, and the money was pouring in with a speed and consistency that both surprised and encouraged me.

Despite how good business was doing, Lennice was still not completely on board. She was fielding phone calls from Pazel Jackson every week, who was trying his best to get me back to the bank. She'd relay his messages to me with her own desire that I'd follow through. I was confused by her adamance. The trucking business was succeeding; we were on an upward swing. It made no sense to walk away from that while it was doing so well. I tried to convince Lennice, to help her see things from my perspective, but she wouldn't budge. She wanted security. She wanted a guarantee.

On my end, I just wanted her to be happy. I not only understood her fears and concerns, but I shared them, too. I tried to come to a compromise, to see if we could find a middle ground that satisfied us both. Perhaps as her own form of concession, she offered to run the business herself while I was in New York. For a while, I thought about her offer. Running the trucking company wasn't an easy thing to do. I had no doubts in her abilities, but it had taken me a long time to get into the swing of things myself. It felt like a lot of responsibility to leave her with, especially considering the fact that she was at home caring for Josh and Justin, who were toddlers at the time. But she insisted she could do it, so eventually, I reluctantly gave in.

Just over a year after I left, I called Pazel Jackson and told him I was coming back to the bank. It was a strange shift for me to go from working for myself, to working in an office again, with and for other people. I'd gotten used to my independence, to being the boss. Although I had great affinity for the bank and the relationships I forged there, I yearned for something else. I wanted nothing more than to be back in the driver's seat of my entrepreneurial endeavors. I wondered constantly how things were going, if operations were running smoothly, and if Lennice was running into any problems.

On Lennice's end, things weren't necessarily as simple as she'd anticipated either. For one thing, she and Eddie butted heads constantly. She hated the smell of his cigarettes, which he smoked constantly, and banished him from coming to the house. Eddie also wasn't taking very well to the fact that Lennice was acting like his boss. He was my older brother after all, and he knew the business far better than she did. Still, she was the one filling out and signing the paperwork, so he had to defer to her, whether he liked it or not. I found my frustrations falling harder on Eddie, expecting him to know and do better.

I'd always heard that doing business with family was risky, and boy did I learn. Though I had the difficult conversations with Eddie when I had to, they never stopped being difficult. Sometimes I had to talk to him about overspending on his expenditures, say no to his request for an advance, or discuss complaints I'd received about his driving. They were awkward conversations before Lennice became involved in the business, but after, they were loaded with even more tension and hurt feelings.

At the same time, Eddie rightfully felt that I was dropping the ball on important business dealings. For one thing, sometimes he wasn't paid on time because I wasn't around to sign his check. I managed to quickly work that kink out by giving Lennice pre-signed checks so that all she'd have to do was fill them out. But sometimes she didn't understand the contracts correctly, and she'd overpay him, resulting in another uncomfortable conversation.

Harmon Transfer Corp. began to experience a downturn. Business was still coming in, but the problems began to pile up, and Lennice wasn't equipped to handle them. I'd go to work, come home exhausted and find a heap of issues waiting for me to deal with. I was no longer there to actively address things as they came up or to manage the company the way my clients had gotten used to. Everything was going haywire and I knew I needed to fix it, fast.

There was a woman I'd worked with on a trucking contract who had offered to take over managing the business end of things while I was in New York. She had years of experience, having done the same things for other companies before. I approached Lennice with the proposal but she shot it down with urgency.

"Absolutely not," she said, leaving no room for discussion. She was completely closed off to the idea, leaving me with very few options. I felt pushed into a corner with every form of recourse I tried being shot down. If I couldn't bring someone else in to run the company while I was in the city, then I'd have to do it myself. Frankly, I didn't even want to be at the bank anyway.

Without consulting Lennice, I quit my job. We'd talked about it until our mouths were dry, and we'd never come up with a solution that would make everyone happy. I didn't have time for conversations anymore. If I didn't act quickly, our ship was bound to sink. When I arrived home the night I quit, Lennice was furious. She felt as though I'd made the decision without consulting her, and she was right. But someone had to right the ship, and that person had to be me. I tried to make her see that though I'd made the decision independently, I'd done it for our family. It wasn't one I'd made with only myself in mind, but for our sons, and the legacy I was trying to leave behind for them.

At this point, in 1992, John was 9, Josh was 4, and Justin was 3. My boys needed me around more than I was able to be there, and I was tired of splitting myself between New York and New Jersey; between my passion and my job. I wanted my business to succeed. I was confident that if I could jump back into it with both feet, we'd have a fighting chance. I didn't know then just how deep in the muck the business had gotten. But I would find out soon enough.

Chapter 6

Growing Pains

Life has a way of humbling you sometimes, of lifting you up to new heights only to cut you off beneath the knees. I learned this lesson the hard way after quitting my job at Chemical Bank in 1992 to try and save my trucking company. It was a pivotal moment in my life, a crossroads that had the power to determine so much about the future, both my own and that of my family. And yet, it was one of the easiest decisions I've ever made.

I could have abandoned Harmon Trucking Corp. and returned to my career in banking. That would have been the safer, more secure route. It was undoubtedly the path my wife would have preferred. But I've never been one to take the easy way out. I knew that the trucking company had the potential to lead my family to the kind of comfort and financial health I imagined for them, but only if I could undo the damage my absence had caused.

Unfortunately, the situation was far worse than I'd anticipated. I wasn't dealing with a leaky ship, as I previously thought, but a sinking one. The problems were coming at me from every direction; client mismanagement, equipment malfunctions, contractor dissatisfaction, and worst of all, cash flow. I felt like I couldn't solve a single issue before it was replaced with an even bigger one.

To complicate things further, the livelihood of my family was dependent on the success of the company. It wasn't like before when we had an alternative income to lean on in case anything went wrong. Lennice wasn't working, and our company was barely bringing in enough capital to offset business expenses and staff salaries, let alone the stack of bills collecting dust on the kitchen counter.

I had an obligation to give my family a good life, and to ensure their needs were being met. But after a few years of trying to keep us afloat, I began to feel hindered in my ability to do just that. Recognizing that the money wasn't coming in fast enough to satisfy the demands of our household as well as the company, I proposed a solution: relocating to Atlanta.

My brother, Dwight first suggested the idea to me. He'd moved there a few years prior with his wife and kids, and he only had good things to say about the city. I'd gone down to visit him a few times, and with each trip, I was able to envision a new life there.

I tossed around the idea in my head for a while, weighing the pros and cons. Knowing the economy in Atlanta was on an upswing, I thought it would be a fresh start for my business and my family. Plus, the cost of living there was much cheaper than it was in Ewing. But at the same time, that meant abandoning the life we'd built, as well as all our friends, family, and community. It also meant pulling the kids out of school, disrupting their routine, and uprooting them from everything they'd grown to know and love.

I approached Lennice with the idea and she seemed just as torn about it as I was. We both knew that something had to change, as our lifestyle was no longer sustainable. But was moving more than 800 miles away the right step to take?

There haven't been many occasions in my life where I felt so thoroughly uncertain about a decision I had to make. I'm a decisive kind of guy, and I tend to trust in my ability to pick a path, and stick to it. But for once, I didn't feel so confident. At the end of the day, as a man of God, I realized it was time to turn to Him for direction.

One Sunday, following morning service, I approached Bishop Roosevelt Butler for some advice. Butler was a small man with a big, welcoming aura which made him easy to talk to and confide in. As we sat down in the pews at the back of the church, I told him about the struggles I was facing with my business. He listened to me, nodding quietly as I explained the predicament I found myself in. He asked me to let him sit with what I'd told him for a while, and he'd get back to me. I was in no rush to figure it out, so I agreed.

A few weeks later, in the middle of the service, Bishop Butler called out my name. "John," he said, his voice booming throughout the building. I looked around, feeling a little unsure of myself, but Bishop Butler was staring right at me, urging me to stand. I pushed myself to my feet, clueless as to what was coming.

"John, the Lord said to activate you." While I heard what he was saying, I stared back at him, dumbfounded. What did that mean? Before I could ask him to clarify, he continued.

"I know things don't make sense right now. You're confused about what to do, and you're feeling lost and uncertain," he shouted, moving closer to where my family sat. "But God is calling on you to stay put, to work through the growing pains. You have a purpose that is far bigger than what you can imagine for yourself. Everything will become clear when the time is right." I felt the hairs on my arm lift as my heart began to beat rapidly in my chest. Lennice and I looked at each other, processing the Bishop's words. I gulped hard, and squeezed Lennice's hand tighter.

"I guess we're staying here," I whispered. Lennice nodded, both of us seemingly accepting his counsel. I felt a sense of calm settle over me, like for the first time in a while, I could fully exhale. Still, I had no idea what to do, or how to address my looming financial crisis. But the anxieties I'd had about the future felt less existential. I regained some of my confidence, and I was prepared to make a decision.

After that prophetic morning, Lennice and I began discussing our options. Now that we knew we wanted to stay in Ewing, the answer seemed glaringly obvious: we had to downsize. Our house was beloved by everyone. It was large and luxurious, and the perfect place to raise a growing family. But frankly, it was costing us too much money. The mortgage, the maintenance, it was all more than we could continue to afford.

We initially purchased the home in 1989 with owner financing. After approaching the lender and explaining my situation, we worked out a plan to deed the house back to them, an agreement that worked out in my favor. At the same time, I had confided in the mother of my old college roommate Greg Foster, transparently sharing the details of our finances. Over the years, Mrs. Foster had become akin to a second mom. Living up to her role, she shared that she had a house in Ewing that had been sitting vacant for a while, and she happily rented it out to us at a discounted rate.

It felt like a Godsend. The house was just a few blocks away from our old house, which meant that our kids could stay in the same school. Even though we were moving to a new house, Lennice and I didn't want the boys to feel their entire lives were being completely uprooted. We tried to preserve their standard of living as much as possible, to help maintain a sense of normalcy. That, however, proved to be a little more challenging.

There were no two ways about it; the new house was a massive downgrade. The exterior was significantly faded and paint was peeling throughout. She'd advised us that it had been vacant for some time, but it was in desperate need of work. Significantly smaller than our previous home where each of the boys had their own room, now, they'd have to share. On the upper floor of the house, the ceiling was so low, I had to stoop down whenever I was up there, as even then, the top of my head skimmed the roof. There was no air conditioning, and only one bathroom.

The new house was undoubtedly an adjustment for us all. I'd grown up in a home where everyone was responsible for carrying our family forward. I wanted my kids to have that same sense of obligation and personal duty. In this case, that meant making small sacrifices to the way we lived. Still, as can be expected, they struggled to adapt to their new dwellings. At the time, John was 12, Josh was 7 and Justin was 6. They were at vulnerable ages, hyper aware of how their friends perceived them.

I didn't know it then, but the boys later told me that they'd often get off the school bus a few stops early to prevent their friends from seeing where they lived. The slightly decrepit condition of the new house embarrassed them.

I could relate. Even for Lennice and I, the move was humbling as hell. I saw the way our peers looked at us, the curiosity and judgment in their eyes. They never asked about our situation, but they didn't have to. Even though the new house was only five minutes away from our old one, the differences were stark.

Lennice did her best to make our family feel comfortable, and to turn the new house into a home. She got right to work painting, hoping to brighten the interior as much as she could. She put in new carpeting, and had air conditioning installed. It's true what they say about a woman's touch; with a few tweaks, she managed to transform the house into a warm and inviting environment, at least marginally easing our transition.

After moving, I focused my attention back on the business. I'd managed to decrease our household expenses, but the real test would be getting Harmon Trucking Corp. back to a profitable place. One of the biggest issues I was dealing with at the time was failing equipment. When I started the company, I'd purchased all used trucks and trailers. Though they'd worked well for the first few years, they were beginning to require regular work and repair, and the costs were adding up quickly.

I needed some extra cash to pay for everything, and to keep my trucks on the road. Without extra funding, operating the business just didn't seem possible. The problem with getting a traditional loan from the bank was that my credit report was marred with a history of slow payments. I'd worked at a bank for years so I knew that any lending authority wouldn't look at that with very much trust.

Around this time, I was catching up with a friend who also happened to be a business owner. Over conversation, he mentioned the New Jersey Economic Development Authority (NJEDA), an organization that had programs for small businesses. The more he told me about it, the more I realized that if I approached them with a thorough and comprehensive business plan, they might be willing to loan me the money I needed. I just had to show them, in clear cut terms, how I planned to spend it, and pay it back. They had a mission to help small businesses thrive and provide small business owners with access to capital, so I felt like I had a good chance.

I quickly got to work putting together my proposal. After spending some time digging into the nitty-gritty of the business' finances, I came up with a number. To get things back on track, I'd need $350,000. I wanted to purchase three refurbished trucks and two trailers, each costing between $40,000-$60,000, along with the equipment we needed that came with warranties. There was roughly $100,000 left over, which would be used as our working capital. I had a list of firm commitments from clients, which basically guaranteed my income.

I felt good about the business plan. I knew I did a good job, and that I'd covered all of my bases while addressing any concerns they might have. When the day of the meeting came, I laid it all out, pitching my proposal with confidence. At the end, they told me that the plan looked good, and that they were interested in lending me the money, but on one condition – I needed to get the Small Business Administration (SBA) to guarantee the loan. The SBA is a federal agency that helps small businesses expand and recover from financial difficulties. After speaking with the SBA, they referred me to Carnegie Bank, who were the potential lenders. If Carnegie Bank agreed with the terms of my business plan, then the SBA would guarantee the loan.

I met with a woman named Marge Callahan at Carnegie, and I pitched my proposal to her. By the end of the meeting, I could tell from the look on her face that she was impressed, but I didn't let myself get too excited just yet.

A few days later, I was sitting at home, going over some business contracts when the phone rang. It was Mrs. Callahan calling to let me know that the SBA was going to guarantee the loan. I was getting the money! I screamed from joy after thanking them profusely, and I hung up the phone to jump around the house in celebration. After *years* of struggling and stressing about how to move forward, it felt like I was finally catching a break. Everything was going to be alright.

Later that day, after I managed to catch my breath and temper my excitement, I called NJEDA to let them know the good news. "My application was approved!" I nearly shouted into the phone. "We can move forward now." I gripped the phone under my chin, as I excitedly hopped from foot to foot. There was silence on the other end of the phone, which made me nervous.

"Hello?" I said, wondering if we'd just lost connection.

"Um, yea, John. I'm here," they said. "Listen, we won't be able to follow through with this. I'm sorry. It's just not in the cards." I waited for a second, hoping they were just pulling my leg. This had to be a joke. When they didn't say anything else, I felt my whole body deflate.

"What do you mean? The SBA guaranteed the loan," I struggled to piece together the words I was hearing as my chest tightened with anxiety. They apologized again, halfheartedly, and told me that it wasn't going to happen before hanging up the phone. I stood there for a few minutes, before slamming the receiver back on the telephone. I didn't understand how this could happen. I'd held up my end of the bargain. I'd done everything they'd asked me to do. And they just reneged on our deal without even offering me the dignity of an explanation. My mood shifted in an extreme way. Earlier, I'd felt on top of the world, like I could do anything, and now, a sense of hopelessness loomed over me.

Was my life just some sick game to them? Had they only made that deal because they didn't believe the SBA would guarantee the loan? I felt like I'd been kicked in the gut. For the next few days, I fell into a deep depression. NJEDA existed to help companies like mine, and yet for whatever reason, I was being denied access to the resources that could save me. It was hard not to take the rejection personally.

A few days later, I called Carnegie Bank back and told them what had happened. After chatting for a little while, they offered to extend their commitment to me, though with some adjustments. Instead of loaning me $350,000, as I'd hoped and planned for, they would give me $100,000. Although $100,000 was substantial, I wasn't sure if it would improve or worsen my situation. It wasn't enough to fix all of my malfunctioning equipment, or to buy new trucks and trailers, but there was still something to be done with the money, if I leveraged it appropriately.

I took some time and deliberated on what to do. Before I could even think of accepting the loan, I had to identify exactly how I'd spend the money. At the very least, I could buy one slightly used truck, and use some of the leftover money to repair the equipment I already had. Anything that remained would be used for our day-to-day operations.

I knew that if I didn't take the loan, the business would be wrapped soon enough. Then, I'd be left combing the job market to find something that made sense for our family. It didn't feel like a sustainable solution, and I went back and forth with myself on what to do. After a few days had passed, I knew I needed to make a final decision. With a sudden sense of urgency, I called Carnegie Bank.

"I can't tell you how grateful I am for your offer," I said, pacing around my kitchen, the phone cord stretching precariously. "Even though it's not the amount I hoped for, we can definitely use it. I'll accept the offer."

In the end, I knew that the loan wouldn't be the thing that saved Harmon Trucking Corp., at least not alone. Despite this, however, I also knew it would at least help ease some of our more urgent concerns, and would pave the way for us to bring in some new business. I tried to see the light; to remain optimistic despite the drastic deviation from the plan. But, as luck would have it, that wasn't in the stars for me, at least not yet.

The day after I closed on the SBA loan and received the money, I went outside to start up one of our existing, working trucks. As I turned the key in the ignition, I heard a screeching sound coming from underneath the hood of the car. The more times I tried to start the vehicle, the worse the sound got until it stopped completely. As I soon discovered, the engine in the truck had failed, throwing yet another wrench in my already busted plans.

It was difficult not to feel like the universe was conspiring against me, like everything that happened was timed meticulously to maximize the effect of the sting. If it wasn't so damaging to my plan, I might have laughed. But I had too much to do, like buying another truck and organizing repairs for everything else. Despite the compounding stresses, I was dedicated to making the business work. I had to. Quitting simply wasn't an option. Even though it sometimes felt like we were trying to make bricks out of straw, I kept going, facing every interruption with as much patience and grit as I could muster.

Afterall, I had a life I had to maintain outside of the business. My boys were growing up fast, and I tried to be as involved in their lives as I could. I knew they were watching me closely, that I was setting an example for them to follow. They were still young, but they'd already inherited my entrepreneurial spirit.

When he was 14, my oldest son, John Jr., enrolled in the Granville Academy, an entrepreneurship program for kids. On the weekends, business leaders and executives would come talk to the youngsters about different aspects of entrepreneurship, exposing them to the endless world of possibilities. They held workshops and activities, and the kids were taught about the fundamentals of starting their own businesses.

The organization was started by a man named Bill Granville, a former Mobil Corporation executive. I'd met Bill back when I worked in New York, and we often made the commute from Trenton to the city together. One Saturday afternoon, when I was dropping John Jr. off, Bill pulled me aside to have a conversation. He told me about another organization he was involved in, one he thought I might be interested in. It was the Metropolitan Trenton African American Chamber of Commerce. The group was still in its infancy, but they were actively looking for more members.

I wasn't immediately sure what the group was all about, but he invited me to attend an upcoming meeting so I could see what kind of work the group was engaged in. When I arrived at the meeting a few days later, there were about 20 of Trenton's business leaders, both Black and white, gathered around the table. I sat back and listened as they discussed their motives and what they hoped to accomplish. They spoke about the challenges Black business owners faced in Trenton, especially when it came to accessing capital. My still-fresh experience dealing with NJEDA came rushing back to me, and I found myself vehemently nodding along in agreement. Trenton has a predominantly African American population, and yet next to no programs existed to help our communities. The group's mission was to change that, and to provide more support, access and opportunities for Black entrepreneurs.

After spending some time listening, I knew I had to get involved. Most of the positions had already been filled, but I was willing to take whatever was available. In the end, the group assigned me the role of chaplain, which I accepted with enthusiasm. The most important thing to me was that I had a seat at that table, and that I could offer my voice, perspective, expertise, and ultimately a hand in making positive changes for Black people in my city.

As I sat there, I suddenly remembered what my pastor had told me not long before. *You have a purpose that is far bigger than what you can imagine for yourself.* It was as if a light had turned on in my life. It was a strange, and eerie feeling, almost as though I was slowly gaining clarity about the struggles I'd faced. I hadn't anticipated this happening, but, suddenly, I had a renewed sense of purpose. Sitting there in that room, surrounded by so many like-minded peers, folks who were also dedicated to empowering our people, I felt like I was exactly where I was meant to be.

Chapter 7

Saving Grace

As a father of three boys who look to me for guidance on what it means to be a man, I have always tried to carry myself with dignity. I strive to be an example they'd be proud to follow. A big and important piece of that puzzle is to be a man of my word. Unfortunately, that isn't always easy or possible. And sometimes, you need to make decisions that don't necessarily reflect the person you try so hard to be.

In 1999, one of those moments happened for me. Financially, my family wasn't doing so hot, and my business, Harmon Transfer Corp., was still struggling to stay afloat. I was running out of ways to get us out of the red zone. Despite all of my efforts, nothing was working. I had creditors who were expecting their money back, but I could never get us stable enough without a new crop of issues entering the fold. The rate at which my equipment was failing outpaced my ability to repair them, and my expenses were becoming exponentially larger, without any growth in my income.

I'd spoken with my colleagues at the Metropolitan Trenton African American Chamber of Commerce about my problems, and one of them introduced me to a bankruptcy attorney named Barry Frost. I set up a time to meet with him to discuss my options, but truthfully, the idea of filing for bankruptcy shook me to my core. I walked into the appointment with Lennice by my side, hesitant and wholly resistant to going down that route. I still had some naive sense of hope that I could turn things around; that I could dig myself out of a hole that was not only getting deeper, but was also quickly filling up with water.

Barry sat on one side of his large wooden desk covered in files and paperwork while Lennice and I sat side by side on the other. I tried my best to hide it, but I was a nervous wreck and could barely sit still. He asked a few questions about my situation, like who I owed money to, and how much. I explained everything to him, from the very beginning of Harmon Transfer Corp., to how we'd ended up in the circumstances we now found ourselves in.

After listening to me intently, he nodded. From the look on his face, it seemed he'd heard this story many times before. He explained to us that there were the two different types of bankruptcy we could choose from: chapter 13 and chapter 7. A chapter 13 bankruptcy allows individuals to set up a court-approved payment plan to slowly pay down their secured debt, like houses and cars, while getting rid of the rest. A chapter 7 bankruptcy, however, protects your assets while discharging your other debts, like personal loans and credit cards. He thought that chapter 7 would be the best choice for us, since most of our problems stemmed from our inability to pay off business-related loans. As he spoke, I dug my fingertips into my temples, trying to massage out the tension building like a storm within my head. Bankruptcy tasted like a bad word. Something we whispered in the dark to avoid the shame and embarrassment associated with it. If I went through with it, I felt as though my entire identity would disappear in a puff of smoke, and that everything I'd accomplished would be forgotten along with it, replaced by this giant, suffocating failure.

Barry could easily see I was wrestling with my own demons, unable to come to terms with my new reality.

"Look, John," he said, folding his hands on his desk while looking at me with a glint of compassion and understanding in his eyes. "I know this is hard. But answer me this question, do you want your life back?"

"Well, of course I do," I said, scratching the side of my head. "It's just that-"

"I know. You feel like claiming bankruptcy is a blight to your character. I get it," he said, nodding his head. "However, it's far more common than you think. You might feel a little uncomfortable at first, but the important thing to remember is that this is a second chance for you. This isn't the end; it's the beginning."

I looked over at Lennice, who had been sitting quietly the entire time, which wasn't exactly in her character. I held her hand and gently squeezed it.

"What do you think, dear?" I asked. I needed her guidance and assurance more than ever.

"He's right, John," she said, cupping my chin in her hand. "We should do this. For our family." Instantly I thought of my boys, and the example I was setting for them. I knew Lennice and Barry were right. It's funny, but when you have kids, your actions become less about what you want and more about what they need. Being a man means taking care of your affairs, even when it's painful. It means being humble enough to admit when you've messed up and having the courage to take accountability, no matter how much shame and embarrassment you feel.

As resistant as I'd been when I first walked in, I agreed to go ahead with filing a chapter 7 bankruptcy. Fortunately, the actual process was relatively simple. Lennice and I gave Barry a full schedule of the debt we owed, and all of the information necessary for him to move forward. It's the aftermath that was difficult.

Bankruptcy was like a scarlet letter that I was forced to wear while I rebuilt my credit, and inevitably, my life. It took years to do and was no easy task, especially since Lennice and I were raising a family; a very expensive endeavor, if there ever was one. Suddenly, everything became even more costly, and I encountered more closed doors than open ones.

But on the flipside of things, it taught our entire family many invaluable lessons. For one we, as a family, had to learn how to manage our money better. This meant we all had to work together to keep our budget balanced, and everyone had a role to play. My kids were at a vital age in their lives, learning the power and importance of money in real time. As much as I would have liked to shield them from the reality of our financial troubles, I knew that it was a temporary situation. The more important aspect of this phase, and the lesson I most wanted my boys to see, was how we responded.

The Bible is filled with many tragedy to triumph stories. Within them are lessons that teach you that if you have faith in God, you'll always find your way through. I've always taught my boys that God will never give you more than you can handle. This point in our lives was no exception. Together, we were determined to work harder and smarter to overcome this storm.

The experience also forced me to look back at my life to reflect on how we'd gotten into this situation. There were a number of times when I'd allowed myself to count my chickens before they hatched. What I mean by this is that I'd depended far too heavily on institutions to support me without getting any guarantees; I'd taken their word at face value (which, I eventually found out, was worthless). I'd been too trusting of the system, and that system screwed me over more times than I could count.

In my blind faith, I failed to come up with any contingency plans. All of those eggs that I'd counted before they hatched, well, I also put them all into one basket. I couldn't go back and change any of that now, but I felt a hell of a lot smarter moving forward.

After filing for bankruptcy, I continued to operate my business, but at a much smaller scale. I still had clients that trusted me with their deliveries, and at least one working truck that I drove myself. As it turned out, this was a good thing because my role with the Metropolitan Trenton African American Chamber of Commerce (MTAACC) was about to expand in a major way.

Since we'd formed MTAACC back in 1997, our board held a luncheon at a local Black restaurant called Maxine's every second Tuesday. There, over some delicious food, we'd go over our plans for increasing membership, and for creating a bigger impact. For two years, we'd been gradually growing our calendar of events, which now included monthly networking luncheons, speaker series, and so much more. We attended community town halls, and actively advocated for Black businesses and business owners as each of us leveraged our unique and specific realm of influence and power however we could. Our efforts, it seemed, had been working, and our membership and attendance numbers began to grow just as fast. It was encouraging to see that the community in Trenton appreciated our efforts, and desired more.

I'd been involved with the organization as a board member and chaplain since 1997, but in 1999, the chair of MTAACC Bill Granville, and the president Burrell Brown, pulled me aside for a conversation. They both had a lot going on outside of the group; Granville (who also ran a youth entrepreneurship group that my boys were involved in) was starting up a charter school in Trenton, and Brown's insurance business had become extremely demanding. Because of their external responsibilities, they had both decided to move on from MTAACC.

I stared at them, surprised by this development. It felt like the group was just beginning to really gain steam. It seemed like an odd time to walk away.

"So what does this mean for the organization?" I asked, looking back and forth between the two men. They looked at each other, and then back at me.

"Well, John, we think you're the right guy to step up and take the lead," Granville said, a serious yet earnest look on his face. I laughed, believing he must have been pulling my leg. When he didn't crack a smile, and neither did Brown, I felt an anxious flutter in my chest.

"Me? You're asking me to take over?" I said, visibly shocked. I didn't feel like I was qualified to be the president of the organization. Sure, I'd run my own business before, but this was different. This wasn't driving trucks and signing sub-contractor cheques. A Chamber of Commerce was a serious undertaking. It required a special kind of knowledge and a particularly astute method of leadership; both of which I didn't feel like I had at the time. I expressed my hesitation to Granville and Brown, that perhaps I wasn't the right person for the job.

"Listen John, we know it's a big leap, but we wouldn't choose you if we didn't believe you could do it," Brown said, leaning forward in his chair. "Trust us, you've got what it takes." Granville nodded his head in agreement.

"And we're still going to be around, brother. Don't worry," Granville said, trying to reassure me. "We'll be here if you need any support. You just turn to us and we've got your back."

I sat back in my chair and thought about it for a few minutes. In the end, I accepted the new position. I loved working with the chamber. I believed so strongly and so completely in our mission to empower Black businesses. I was a business owner myself, and I knew firsthand how challenging it was to try to obtain support we offered from the institutions that were meant to help us.

I mightn't have had experience in a leadership position like this before, but what I did have was passion and the desire to see the chamber grow. Plus, I had the support of two fully fledged pioneers, men I could lean on for advice and guidance whenever I needed it.

After speaking with Granville and Brown, I reached out to some of the other board members of MTAACC to see how they felt about me becoming president. I wanted to ensure that the core group of people we had still felt committed to the group, now with me as their new leader. Many of them pledged their support, letting me know that they approved of my promotion.

At the time, one of our members, Stephanie Barrington Jones, was an executive at Fleet Bank. The bank had a vacant second floor which she provided for us to use as a working space. I had my own private office where I quickly began spending all of my time. For the first few months after I became president, I dedicated every free moment I had to familiarizing myself with the ins and outs of running a Chamber of Commerce.

I read our bylaws front to back and several times over, ensuring I thoroughly understood every line. I learned everything I could about our members, our operations, and our relationships with other organizations in Trenton. I attended any and all business-related meetings that occurred in the community, and introduced myself to make sure all of the important business players were aware of my new role.

As president of MTAACC, I was given a position as a board member of the Mercer County Chamber of Commerce, which was also located in Trenton. At the time, the organization had been in operation for nearly 70 years. It was an incredible learning opportunity for me to watch firsthand how the group governed itself, ran their board meetings, planned events, developed a budget, and so much more. I was an eager student, actively taking note of what I thought worked well, and how I could use those learned skills to strengthen MTAACC's own mission. I gained an even better understanding of how to network and leverage relationships, while ensuring our organization was fully utilizing the resources we had within our ranks.

Since we weren't just a Chamber of Commerce, but specifically a Black Chamber of Commerce, I also sought out information on the history of Black businesses in the U.S. As it currently stood, there were no organizations within New Jersey that advocated for the economic empowerment of Black folks. What we had were the NAACP, the Urban League, and several other organizations that championed Black folks socially and across other spheres. But economically, there was a huge gap in influence. This vacuum was even more stark considering Black people made up 20 percent of the population in Mercer County.

I learned about the National Black Chamber of Commerce, which inevitably introduced me to the vast sphere of Black chambers that existed across the country; nearly 150 of them. There were dozens of meetings and conferences to attend and information to read.

Almost immediately, I was introduced to the teachings of Booker T. Washington, the founder and leader of the National Negro Business League (better known today as the National Business League). Founded in 1900, the NNBL advocated for the economic development of Black communities and for creating a more equitable society where Black people had more and better access to opportunities.

I studied the organization's history, and how Washington had managed to achieve so much success for his time. But it wasn't lost on me that we still hadn't accomplished many of the things that Washington had been advocating for upwards of five decades earlier. Still, I was empowered by his teachings, and fired up to make MTAACC's influence stronger and more impactful.

About a year into my tenure, in 2000, I met a man named Bill Brooks, who was President of the Regional Alliance of Small Contractors. Bill worked with construction companies in New Jersey to build their capacities. Upon meeting, we both had the same idea, that perhaps economic empowerment for Black folks required a more holistic approach. In Trenton, we had the Urban League, the NAACP, the Concerned Pastors (a religious organization that sought to unify the voice of the church on critical social, political and economic issues), and MTAACC. If all of our organizations worked together, Bill and I felt confident that we could achieve far more than any of us could alone.

We began meeting with members of each organization regularly at a local soul food restaurant to discuss the possibility of us creating a cohesive plan to economically advance the Black community. We called the idea 'Empowerment 2000.' Each group would have a specific function in the grand scheme of our plan. Concerned Pastors would identify people within the community who needed help with finding employment, or needed support for their businesses. The Urban League would help with workforce training, and assisting people in professional development and coaching. The NAACP would deal with any injustices that took place within the community, including in the workplace. And finally, MTAACC would be the advocate attending political and business-centered meetings to ensure Black businesses were being fairly considered and promoted for business contracts and opportunities.

I thought the model was brilliant and something that could create real and enduring change. I truly believed that if we could implement Empowerment 2000, and put it into action, Trenton would be the tip of the iceberg. It was a plan that, if followed correctly, could be executed in any Black community across the country.

After a few weeks of discussing, tweaking, and debating roles and responsibilities, we came to an agreement on a plan of action. We organized a day to meet at the restaurant to sign off on the terms of employment. When the day finally arrived, Bill and I arrived early and ordered a few plates of fried fish.

Our food came, and went, but the other organizing members never did. As it turned out, we wouldn't hear from any of them again. Despite how eager they'd seemed to get on board with the plan, we soon realized that they weren't as committed to the idea of empowerment as we were. And as I'd eventually realized, many folks in positions of authority within our communities were far more self-serving than they were community serving; an unfortunate reality that pushed me to fight even harder for my people.

I encountered similar challenges over and over again as I got deeper into my role as president. As much as many people spoke about advancement, progress, and empowerment, these were simply buzzwords for them. In their eyes, it was merely empty jargon or fleeting campaign slogans. When the time came to truly act on our commitments, I discovered that many folks would actually be working against our efforts, instead of for them.

At this time, I was balancing my role as president, and the flood of obligations that entailed, all while still running my trucking business. Even though Harmon Transfer Corp. was operating at limited capacity, the compounding responsibilities I now carried meant I was burning the candle at both ends. I'd spend my days working at the chamber, and my nights fulfilling deliveries and shipments. I was being torn between two marriages: my old trucking business, and my new, exciting venture with MTAACC.

The thing was, my job as president of the chamber didn't bring in very much, if any money at all at first. With a family to support, and three growing boys, it was a difficult balancing act, and one I didn't always succeed at. I was putting in dozens of hours every week, dedicating most if not all of my free time to growing the organization, so it was only a matter of time before I knew that I'd need to be paid for my work with the chamber.

A few board members, Tracey Syphax, Linda Robinson, and Stephanie Barrington Jones, were all huge advocates on my behalf. When we began having this conversation, it was around the time when memberships were set to be renewed. This meant we'd have to inform our members of this new implementation.

Before announcing the change, we'd had over 100 members. After the announcement, our numbers whittled down to just 32 individuals. This was caused, in part, because now, some were seeking to establish a base line of compensation. It was a disheartening development, and one I hadn't quite anticipated. When I'd agreed to take over the position, I did so with the understanding that I was going to be in charge of an organization that was trying to empower and uplift the Black business community in Trenton. Yet somehow, it seemed that my presence was ruffling a lot of feathers. Every effort I made to move us forward came up against resistance.

Even within our organization, there were a few arrangements I identified that did more to hinder our mission than further it. For example, my predecessors had structured an arrangement wherein the Mercer County Chamber of Commerce received 80% of MTAACC's membership dues. This left very little for our operations, and practically nothing for member salaries. I was determined to put an end to this, and to keep our organization's contributions within our own hands.

Unsurprisingly, not everyone on the Mercer County Chamber (or even on our own) was on board with this change. Moreover, there were some Black leaders that balked at my plans to pursue a more independent relationship with the Mercer Chamber. As things currently stood, we were hustling backwards. We worked hard to grow our membership, and yet we barely experienced the fruit of our labor; a reality that I found impossible to accept.

Thanks to the support of other board members, we were eventually able to keep MTAACC's financial resources within our organization, and I began to earn a salary, which substantially helped facilitate the work I was doing.

In 2001, I decided to expand my network even further to see how I could possibly connect MTAACC to more chambers across the country. I'd first been introduced to the National Black Chamber of Commerce, founded by Harry Alford and Kay DeBow in 1993, when I first became president. My relationship with them up until that point had been mostly educational; they'd connected me with resources and information. But now, I needed to work towards forging a deeper relationship.

One day, I called Harry and introduced myself. I told him about MTAACC, and the work we were trying to do in New Jersey. He was excited by our progress and my enthusiasm, and he invited me to attend an event in Washington with the U.S. Chamber of Commerce. There, I met dozens of Black chamber presidents, and learned more about how they ran their organizations, eagerly accepting their guidance and advice. That day, in a room surrounded by advocates all fighting for the advancement of Black businesses, I found myself.

I'd entered an entirely new playing field, and had positioned myself in an arena far more vast than I'd anticipated. Even though I'd always hoped my work could have a larger, more far-reaching impact, suddenly, it no longer seemed like such a daunting and impossible task. After connecting with Harry and the many other inspiring leaders that were in attendance, Trenton seemed like such a small circle of influence. That night, I began plotting out the first steps toward a much bigger organization: a state-wide Chamber of Commerce.

Chapter 8

Snakes in the Chamber

When you enter into the important work of trying to change the conditions of your people, you might, like me, encounter a frustrating obstacle in your path. You discover that people from your own community will try to sabotage you, and install impossible hurdles to sully your name and your mission.

From the jump, I'd anticipated having to face pushback from the white community in Trenton, and I did. On more than a few occasions, especially in the beginning of my tenure as president of MTAACC, I was forced to answer the question, "why do we need a *Black* chamber?" over and over again. Every time I was faced with this absurd inquiry, I recoiled internally. I'd attend networking events with corporate representatives from all over the state where many of the people I'd met and introduced myself to on several occasions pretended as if it were the first time. They'd smile at me smugly, asking what I did, as if I hadn't explained the chamber and our mission to them before.

These microaggressions were a nuisance, but because I'd expected them, it made it easier to swallow. What I hadn't anticipated though was encountering so many enemies within my own community; a realization that proved to be far more painful.

In the early years of MTAACC, Bill Granville, the former CEO of the organization, had moved on to build one of the first charter schools in Trenton. Bill was an impressive guy who commanded respect from everyone around him. As a former vice president of Mobil Oil, he'd traveled all over the world and spoke several languages. His son played for the Cincinnati Bengals, and Bill himself was an avid golfer with a country club membership. He sat in rooms and at tables that most Black people weren't invited to, and he did it all on the back of his own hard work.

As a sort of nod to the work we were doing, he made me a member on the school's board. This was a strategic position that allowed me to advocate on behalf of Trenton's many Black businesses to ensure they played a role in the construction and renovation of the school. It was a lucrative project that came with a nearly 20 million dollar budget.

At the outset, we were assured that Black folks, a demographic that made up more than half of Trenton's population, would be involved. Yet, when I attended board meetings and listened as presenters attempted to sell us all on future plans, I'd be the lone voice in the room asking about minority participation. The school was being founded by a Black man, yet Black participation and involvement was notably lacking. Despite my persistent questioning about how Black folks would be included, I never received any real, concrete answers. They'd tiptoe around the topic, claiming they would address the matter as the project advanced.

One night, after I'd attended one of these vague, promised-filled meetings, I tossed and turned in my bed, unable to sleep. I'd been involved with the MTAACC for a few years now, and believed so strongly in its mission. This charter school was the perfect opportunity to uplift Black businesses and help fulfill our purpose. There were millions of dollars in checks to be cashed, I felt it in my gut that we wouldn't be getting any of them. That night, I reconciled that my presence on the board was symbolic; a means of selling the lie of Black participation. And I didn't want to be part of something that felt like a betrayal of my people or my role as president of the chamber. Too often, I witnessed Black folks getting played by promises made and broken with an ease that made me uncomfortable.

I sat up in my bed and turned on the lamp. I picked up the notepad and pen that I kept by my bedside table and began scribbling out my resignation from the board. As I penned the last words of my letter, I felt a shudder of relief.

The following morning, I called Bill and told him that we needed to talk. When we got together, I handed him the resignation letter. He stared down at it, his eyes widening in shock the further down the page he got. After reading my letter to completion, he looked up at me with his eyes that searched my face for answers.

"John, what in the world do you think you're doing?" he asked, clearly angry. "Why are you doing this?" The resignation had caught him completely off guard. I shrugged my shoulders.

"I know you're upset Bill, but this was an easy decision for me," I said, standing firm. "I'm not comfortable being associated with this project anymore." He shook his head in disbelief.

"But why? I don't understand," he said, pacing back and forth. I sighed, motioning to the letter in his hand.

"It's all in there, Bill. I have a responsibility to my members. This is so much bigger than you and I, you know that." Well, at least I hoped he did. Reluctantly, he accepted my resignation. Leaving our meeting, I held onto the hope that, despite my departure from the school's board, we would continue a cordial and respectful professional relationship. Afterall, he was still involved with the chamber, and despite how bitterly the charter project had gone, at least in my mind, we were still playing for the same team.

Soon enough, I learned the hard way just how naive I was being. I didn't announce my resignation, but the news trickled out. Just as quickly, I began hearing rumors about myself, spread by some local preachers connected to Bill. "John's not the go along and get along type of guy," they were saying. "He's a problem. I'd be careful about having him around." It hurt to hear what people were saying about me, and to see folks I'd had decent working and personal relationships with begin to distance themselves. But at the same time, I had no regrets about my decision. In fact, it only opened my eyes to many of the realities I'd been blind to, or rather, chose to avoid. The experience taught me that some people will use the facade of serving others to further their own agendas.

I tried to carry that lesson forward as I continued building the chamber, and developing my plans for a statewide organization. I also used my time to focus on deepening the relationships I had with other groups, like the National Black Chamber. Unlike some of the folks in Trenton who were actively trying to smear my name, the founders of the National Black Chamber, Harry Alford and Kay Debow, saw something in me. Harry came out to New Jersey to personally teach me how to, as he called it, 'hunt and kill' when speaking to corporations about sponsorships, and applying for support. Harry and Kay believed in what I was trying to do, so much so that I began traveling with them for conferences both domestically and abroad. We journeyed to different parts of Georgia and Florida, even traveling as far as

Ghana and Cuba. It was invigorating, and I saw the impact of their work firsthand.

Through the National Black Chamber, I also met others who helped guide me along my path. Larry Ivory, who headed the Illinois State Black Chamber, which had more than 20 chapters, taught me many best practices. He shared with me a book he wrote called *Blueprint for Success*, which explained how to structure and run an effective chamber. I read it, cover to cover several times, highlighting the parts that felt especially important, leaving my own jumble of notes and edits in the margins. There was also Sherrie Gilchrist, who invited me to visit her in Chattanooga where she was running a very effective and influential chamber. I spent a few days out there with her, listening to her story about how she'd started the organization, and the programs they'd implemented since then.

In 2002, about a year after getting involved with the National Black Chamber, the U.S. Chamber of Commerce, the largest business federation in the country, invited me to Washington, and asked me to bring along other Black Chamber presidents, too. I invited Clay Hammond, president of the African American Chamber of Philadelphia, and Henry Johnson, who I'd helped found the Northern New Jersey Black Chamber.

Located right across from Lafayette Square, the three of us arrived at the chamber. They led us to a huge boardroom, with a long table in the center that was scattered with pamphlets and information packets. They proceeded to give us a thorough history of the U.S. Chamber of Commerce, from its inception in 1912 until the present day. At the end of the presentation, they asked us if we'd like to join. I felt giddy with excitement. It felt like an opportunity of a lifetime, first to get this exclusive introduction to the group, and now to be invited in.

"Well, how much is it to join?" I asked. By now, I'd become very familiar with the process of these organizations. They told me that it would cost $750 a year. Without a second thought, I pulled out a credit card from my wallet and slid it across the table.

"Sign me up!" I said, enthusiastically. I looked at Clay and Henry, expecting them to do the same. They watched me with a bit of surprise on their faces.

"Well, I've got to think about this a while," Clay answered, looking at Henry, who nodded in agreement.

"Yeah, me too. I'll have to get back to you," Henry said. Now I was the one with the look of surprise and shock on my face. *What's there to think about?* I thought to myself. *This was a no brainer.* But I kept my opinions to myself. We all headed back home after that, me to Trenton, Clay to Philadelphia, and Henry to Newark. I followed up with them a week after getting home, but I never heard from them.

After returning home from Washington, I felt energized and ready to take the chamber to the next level. But in 2004, we were faced with a new and unexpected predicament. Fleet Bank, where MTAACC operated out of, was purchased by Bank of America. As such, they were set to close their offices and relocate. At first, we were told that we'd have the opportunity to move our operations to their new building, just a few blocks away. But it soon became clear that Bank of America had no intention of making space for us in their branch.

To make matters worse, the Bank of America property managers wanted us out immediately. I tried to speak some sense into them, to get them to let us stay at least until we could find somewhere else to relocate to. But they weren't hearing it. At that exact time, my dear Aunt Lorine had passed, and I was devastated. Even though I didn't get to see her as often as I would've liked, she was one of my favorite aunts. Every time I visited her out in Virginia, she had something delicious waiting for me. Chicken and dumplings, sweet custards, bread pudding. I never knew what would be there, but I knew I couldn't wait to eat it.

I told the property managers at Bank of America that I had to drive out to Virginia to attend her funeral, and would have to deal with moving MTAACC's things elsewhere when I returned. But when I got back, I discovered that they'd taken the liberty of discarding our belongings in my absence. I was enraged by their lack of compassion, but I didn't have time to fixate. I needed to get our organization resituated immediately.

I knew some folks over at Roma Savings Bank, so I reached out to them to explain our predicament. Peter Verso, who was the chairman of the bank's board, told me that they had a space they would be happy to lend us. We quickly shifted our things into the new office space. It was a touch smaller than the one we had at Fleet, but it worked. We had several offices, including one I would use to start building the state organization. Our group happily settled into our new digs, and our work continued.

Professionally, things in my life were progressing at an even and smooth pace. I was leading MTAACC, and on the board of several others. I was also still running Harmon Transfer Corp., which continued to operate on a much smaller scale. The chamber had agreed to start paying me a salary in 2001, but I didn't see much of that money until around 2004 when we finally began to bring in a sizable revenue. By then, our family was doing pretty well financially, too. It hadn't been easy, but we'd managed to get ourselves out of the red. We were slowly building our way back to a place of normalcy and ease.

Early that year, we'd made enough money for me to buy Lennice a new car, a Volkswagen Jetta. She'd sold her other car to help us afford the down payment when we purchased our big, fancy house in Ewing.

Since then, she'd struggled along with an old, busted vehicle we bought for dirt cheap.

I arranged to get the car delivered to the house on her birthday, with a big red ribbon placed right on the hood. When it arrived, I called her outside.

"Lennice! Come out here for a minute, I need you to see something," I said sheepishly, barely able to conceal my excitement. My boys stood near the car smiling, waiting to see their mom's reaction.

When Lennice stepped outside, her mouth dropped open as she screamed out in excitement.

"John!" she squealed, grabbing my arm. "Is it mine? Is this *my* car?" I laughed and wrapped my arms around her waist, kissing her softly.

"It's yours, my dear. Happy birthday!" Lennice kissed me quickly and ran towards the car to get a closer look. I watched as she and the boys inspected the brand-new vehicle, gushing over the soft seats and the shiny exterior.

Our family absolutely struggled for a while. Lennice hadn't been thrilled when I became president of MTAACC, but she'd slowly warmed up to the new reality of our life. By this time, our marriage had faced so much turbulence from career changes, a failing business, bankruptcy, and money troubles. We'd gone through the ringer, and our marriage hadn't survived unscathed. But we knew that if we were going to make it, we'd have to work together. It meant having to put aside whatever issues we had for the sake of the bigger picture: our family. Now, we were coming out the other side stronger—financially and emotionally.

By 2005, the boys were barely boys anymore. John Jr. was 22 and had long crossed that threshold into adulthood. Josh was 17 and Justin was 16. I was always pretty open with my boys, so they knew about the difficulties our family faced after the bankruptcy. It hadn't been easy for them; our money troubles coincided with that slippery time in a boy's life when they started to discover their personal style and showed a greater interest in how they dressed. All of those were expensive, especially for growing boys who seemed to outgrow things the second you bought them. But they'd been patient and understanding with Lennice and me, and we were deeply appreciative for that.

Don't get me wrong, they raised a fuss every now and then about things they couldn't have, like all boys do. But it could've been much worse. Around this time, Josh had started pleading with me to buy a new house. We'd been in Mrs. Foster's little home in Ewing for years, and even though we'd put a lot of work into transforming it into a far nicer home than we'd found it, Josh still felt we were due for an upgrade. And I didn't disagree.

To be fair, I was making enough to get us a bigger spot. Plus, I'd made some crucial connections in my time at the chamber. Tim Losch, who I served on the board of the Mercer County Chamber of Commerce with, was the President of Yardville Bank. I shared with Tim that I was thinking of purchasing a new home, and he told me that he'd work with me to make it happen. He advised me to speak with Nina Melker, a loan officer at the bank who I was also connected with through the chamber. When I approached Nina with my proposal, she nodded knowingly.

"I spoke with Tim, John," she said, handing me a set of forms. "Here's the application. Fill it out and go find a place." After getting everything filled out, I set Josh up with the important task of finding us the right house. He'd been the dominant voice pushing for this, so I wanted him to be involved in the process as much as possible.

At first, we tried to find a place in Ewing so we could stay connected to the community we'd built there, but we quickly discovered that all of the houses we wanted in the county were out of our budget. Trenton, however, had exactly what we were looking for. Almost immediately after starting our search, we found a beautiful home in West Trenton on Riverside Avenue, just a few blocks away from the house my family lived in when I was a teenager.

The house was huge. It had six bedrooms and four bathrooms, which meant the boys could finally get their own rooms, and we'd all have more space to roam. As Josh and I wandered through the house during a showing, we both felt it – this was the one. I could vividly see my family living there. I could see us all gathered around the kitchen island on Sunday mornings, laughing and joking around as we fried up slabs of bacon, and spread butter on slightly burnt slices of toast. I saw Lennice decorating a Christmas tree in the spacious and brightly lit living room, as the boys lounged on the couch.

Once those images entered my mind, I was sold. I needed to have this house. The only problem was that Lennice wasn't exactly on the same page. She agreed that we could use a bigger house, but she had no desire to move to Trenton. She wanted to stay in Ewing, and I understood why. We'd built a life there. It was where our community was, where we raised our kids and where they attended school. Even though Trenton and Ewing were less than five miles apart, to Lennice it felt much further. Though I understood her position, I tried my best to persuade her to see my vision.

"Listen Len, this house is a really great opportunity for us," I pleaded. "If you just come see it, I know you're going to love it. It's the perfect house for our family." Lennice looked at me, her big, curious eyes inspecting my face. I could tell just by looking at her that she was trying to suss out how serious I was, and how invested I was in making this move.

Despite her initial reluctance, Lennice eventually softened to the idea and we bought the house. The night we closed, Josh and I decided to spend the night there. The house was completely empty, and every room bare as a bone. But it didn't matter. We set up our pillows and blankets on the floor and camped out.

A few days later, the rest of the family (and all of our furniture) moved in, too. Once again, Lennice got straight to work transforming the beautiful house into a comfortable and cozy home. She always had a special knack for decorating, and she could make any space feel warm and inviting. This house was no exception.

As a new chapter of our lives began, another one came to an end. That very year, I made the difficult but necessary decision to close Harmon Transfer Corp. I'd had the company for nearly 15 years; in so many ways, it was like one of my kids. By then, it was clear to me that my life was just heading in a different direction. I was heavily involved with MTAACC and making plans to develop the statewide organization, as well. With the trucking business still in the picture, I was trying to serve two very different masters, dividing my time in a way that didn't make sense, and no longer benefited each other.

Still, I struggled with my goodbyes. As I began winding down operations, I was swept back into the past, and into the long hours I'd spent with the old trucking guys who'd taught me so much about being a man. Since getting involved with the chamber, I hadn't been very present at the Saturday morning diner meets where we used to gather, exchange stories, work on our trucks, and prepare for the upcoming week. The few times I was able to make it out, it was clear to the others that I had one foot in and one foot out.

For instance, I wasn't in my casual work clothes like the rest of them, but in a suit (which had become my de facto uniform after shifting to a more business-forward environment working in a chamber). And I wasn't about to fix any trucks in that get-up. Gradually, my visits became shorter and shorter. I'd usually hang around for breakfast or a cup of tea, then head right back out to my office. When I told the guys I was closing the business, none of them were surprised.

After shutting down my company, I was completely focused on building and expanding the chamber. By then, the organization had been in operation since 1997, and I'd been the president since 1999. For that entire duration, we'd been in the papers nearly every week, either promoting our events or advocating for change. We were impossible to ignore, even if you tried. Yet within its eight years of operation, we'd never managed to get before Trenton's mayor Doug Palmer, and it wasn't due to a lack of trying.

Since I'd become president, I'd tried fruitlessly to arrange a meeting. Trenton had been experiencing an economic renaissance with many massive, lucrative developments being built throughout the city (a $60 million baseball stadium, a $40 million arena, a $63 million hotel, and a $120 million tunnel). And from the looks of it, there were many more in the works.

I wanted to ensure that the Black mayor of our majority Black city was assigning as many of these projects to Black companies. To me, it seemed like a no-brainer. Why wouldn't our leader want to partner with an organization working day and night to empower Black folks? And yet, I could never seem to get in front of him.

In 2004, I attended a city council meeting where I was able to get my name on the docket. When it was my time to speak, I laid it all out.

"I'm the president of the Metropolitan Trenton African American Chamber of Commerce," I said, bending down to speak into the microphone. "My organization actively advocates for Black businesses in our city. And for years, I've been trying to get in front of the mayor, to partner with him to bring our mission of economic empowerment for Black folks to fruition. Surely, as a Black mayor, that mission should appeal to him. And yet, I can't seem to get in the same room as him. Why is that?"

The council stared at me a little surprised, but they quickly sprang into action, assuring me that the mayor's office would be in touch in no time. A few days later, I finally got the call. When I met with Doug Palmer, I told him that I really wanted him to meet some of the members of our organization. Collectively, we hoped to foster a relationship that could be of great benefit to both parties, him and us. He agreed, and a meeting was set.

When I went back to the group to tell them the news, they were ecstatic. We were full of hope and expectation, imagining the possibilities of what we could accomplish with the mayor on our team. When the day of the meeting came, myself and approximately 25 members of MTAACC headed over to city hall. We were guided into a conference room where we waited, like eager school kids, for Doug to arrive.

But pretty soon, I got the feeling the whole thing was more posturing than anything else. The mayor showed up nearly 40 minutes late for our meeting. When he did arrive, he told us that he only had ten minutes to spare. The mood had understandably dimmed a little, but I tried to keep everyone excited and to make the most of the little time we had left.

Our organization had come up with a proposal we hoped to present. We wanted to erect signs on all of the gateways entering into the city to pay tribute to Doug Palmer as mayor, and established our organization as sponsors. We'd already completed the design and were willing to pay for the whole thing. Doug's Public Works Director, Eric Jackson was there, and was responsible for carrying out activities like the one we were proposing. Doug directed him to get on it right away, and we got him all of the information he needed.

We agreed to meet with the mayor every quarter to discuss our progress and to see how things were developing. When the next meeting rolled around, nearly three months later, the mayor never showed. Such became the pattern with him missing the one after that, and the one after that one, too. On the fourth meeting, almost a year since we'd first proposed our initiative, he finally made an appearance. But since our very first meeting, nothing had actually happened. The signage never went up, and none of our members were able to engage in any discussions about opportunities with his team over that period. When we asked the mayor about the status of the signage, he quickly got on his phone and called the Public Works Director, urging him to 'handle it asap'.

The thing is, I'm no sucker, and I can tell when I'm being played. I saw right through his phony phone calls and false promises. I watched him feign urgency and care for our organization and all of the hard work we were doing, something in me shifted. I was tired of watching this scenario play out over and over again. Even with a Black mayor at the helm, we were still getting the short end of the stick. I knew what I had to do: I was going to run for mayor.

Even to me, the decision seemed a little crazy. I'd never been involved in politics before, and I knew as well as anyone else that I wasn't the most popular guy in Trenton. I'd made my fair share of enemies when I refused to go along with Bill Granville's charter school, even though my refusal came from a place of principle. The thing is, you don't always get to write your own story, especially when you're up against a guy with much more clout than you.

When most folks think of community empowerment and fighting for the betterment of the people, they aren't usually imagining a business guy in a suit. I get it. Corporations and capitalism are the tools of Republicans and anti-progressives, which are often perceived as one and the same. But economic empowerment is fundamental to Black liberation. As a businessman whose mission is to empower Black businesses and entrepreneurs with access to resources and opportunities, I am directly advocating for Black power. Unfortunately, that's not an easy sell.

Still, none of that factored into my decision. I knew that if given the opportunity, I could make a bigger impact than some of the announced candidates, the current mayor included. The problem was, Doug Palmer was a very popular guy. He'd been elected mayor in 1990, and every year since. Over time, I got the impression that he liked being the only Black guy at the table, and it didn't seem like he was willing to make space for any more of us to join him. I desperately wanted to change that. My first plan of action was to connect with some out-of-state friends who had experience running campaigns. My friend, Ernie Jones, was a big player in New York politics before he and his wife Nancy relocated to Atlanta. I called him and he encouraged me to reach out to a political consultant named Roland Washington.

Roland and I met up in Trenton and he set me up with some resources to get started. He gave me a list of articles and books to read to suss out my resolve and to ensure I knew what I was getting myself into. Then, he told me to establish a 'kitchen cabinet' of trusted advisors composed of folks I could rely on to have my back over the next few months.

Once I'd assembled my team, it was time to figure out my campaign platform. I knew that I wanted accountability to be a policy, something that I identified as missing from the current mayor's office. In addition, I always felt that Trenton didn't feel like a true state capital, despite our city playing such an important role in both New Jersey and American history. Trenton was a leader in the Industrial Revolution. We supplied the steel that built both the Golden Gate and Brooklyn Bridge. We provided textiles, fabrics, and many other important resources to the entire country. The Battle of Trenton, fought in our very city, was one of the most important in the American Revolutionary War.

I didn't think our current mayor was doing nearly enough to leverage our history or to encourage tourism to our city. Trenton had *just* gotten its first major hotel, the Marriott, a few years prior. My strategy was to identify all of the ways that Trenton was underperforming, and then show voters exactly how I'd change that if I was voted into office. It was a bold stance to take, but we managed to garner a lot of support, even from players outside of the city who agreed with my platform.

Nonetheless, running an election campaign was no easy task. I was working 12 hour days, nearly every day. Fundraising was a huge and time-consuming task, but one that required daily attention. Every day, my campaign manager sat me down for 'call-time', which is exactly what it sounds like. Two hours a day were reserved for calling potential donors, asking for their monetary support. This was a non-negotiable aspect of the campaign, and possibly one that I hated the most. I never got comfortable with the act of asking people for money. Something about the whole thing made me feel awkward and uneasy. Despite that, my efforts were effective, and we were able to raise more than $200,000 in less than six months, which was no small feat.

Lennice wasn't too enthusiastic about me running for mayor, but at least in the beginning, she attended most of my events. By the end though, her support had sort of petered out, a fact that broke my heart and deeply impacted our relationship.

My competitor, Doug, was married to a very prominent and successful white woman, who also happened to be extremely kind. However, she didn't appear much in public with him, which I felt provided us an opportunity to contrast that by presenting my own strong, Black family unit every chance we got. I pleaded with Lennice to see how important her presence was on the campaign trail, but it was to no avail. Still, I was happy to at least have my boys by my side, especially Josh. He could often be found amidst the volunteers, handing out flyers and pamphlets, encouraging people to vote for me.

The day of the election passed by in a blur. We began the day canvassing the neighborhoods where we thought I had the best chance of leading the polls. I spoke with voters in the hopes of encouraging them to elect me. Josh rode around on the back of a truck with a bullhorn, shouting 'Vote for John Harmon! He's not a politician, he's a businessman!' I got a big kick out of that.

By the evening, my entire family, along with all of our volunteers and campaign supporters were gathered at the office as the votes were being tallied. Things looked promising in the beginning as I was leading in West Ward One after the early votes were announced. But as more and more votes started coming, it was clear I wasn't going to come out on top. In the end, Doug won the election for a fifth term. Importantly though, he won that election with a much smaller margin than his previous run, something I will happily take responsibility for. At the end of the night, I went out and made my concession speech.

"'Unfortunately, we didn't win this time around," I said, staring into the small crowd, and occasionally glancing at the TV cameras. "But we still showed up, and we made this city proud. More importantly, we made ourselves proud by showing the residents of Trenton that there is an alternative that really, genuinely cares about them." I noticed many wet eyes in the room, which warmed my heart in unexpected ways.

"We came up short, but that's okay. Tomorrow, right after I call Doug Palmer and congratulate him for his win, I'll be right back to work at the chamber. Even though I didn't win the election, I'm still going to fight for this city. I'm still committed to making Trenton a better place for us all. And that's a promise."

And honestly, that was the truth. I ran for mayor because I genuinely wanted to make a difference in my city. I love Trenton. My dedication didn't falter in the least following my loss. In fact, if anything, I was even more determined to make an impact. And somehow, I felt more equipped than ever before.

The campaign immensely improved my public speaking skills, and I felt like a stronger, more well-rounded leader. Being immersed in politics, even for just that shadow of time, helped me view my work with the chamber in a new light. I learned how to more effectively connect the dots between policy and economic opportunity, and to become a more potent advocate for my community. The whole experience also gave me a new layer of influence that I hadn't necessarily had before. Many corporate leaders and people of influence suddenly recognized me, and even respected me.

In addition, the election experience opened my eyes to the necessity of a Black *statewide* Chamber of Commerce. Local chambers, like MTAACC, were vital, no doubt, But those chapters needed to exist in tandem and underneath larger ones to truly expand their circle of influence.

I wanted to develop that chamber; the one that would benefit and further all of the Black businesses and owners in New Jersey. I saw the work and impact that other statewide organizations were having, and I wanted those same opportunities for my people, as well. For years, I'd been slowly plotting out the steps I needed to make my ideas a reality, but before I could act on those plans, I needed to find the right folks to take over my role at MTAACC as I began to transition out.

There was a man I'd met in the early years of my presidency named Herb Ames who oversaw the Economic Development department of Mercer County. The first time we met, I'd gone over to his office with my colleagues Tracy Syphax and Sherwood Brown to discuss creating a partnership between our organization and Mercer County. For whatever reason, something about Herb rubbed me the wrong way. I seemed to have elicited a similar reaction, because during our very first interaction, we nearly got into a physical altercation. After that initial meeting, we avoided each other for some time. While MTAACC and Mercer County were able to forge a partnership, Herb worked mostly with Tracy and Sherwood.

As more time passed, we eventually got to a better place. We began to understand each other better and our relationship improved. It wasn't great, but we were cordial with each other. I could see that he, like me, wanted to create change, so even if my personal feelings towards him were less than ideal, I was willing to put those aside for the sake of the greater good.

When 2006 rolled around, we suddenly found MTAACC without a chair when Barbara Armand, the woman who had previously been serving, left for California to take care of some family matters following the death of her brother. She didn't know when she'd be back, but a precarious situation was taking place in the chamber which needed my immediate attention.

Before Barbara left for California, I had been away for a few weeks connecting with the National Black Chamber of Commerce in Washington. When I finally returned home, I conducted my usual tour of duty, checking that all departments were functioning well. This included a weekly meeting with our bookkeeper.

During this meeting, she told me that she had three checks that I'd signed, totalling $14,000, and she needed to know what they were for. To my surprise, I didn't know either. As we started investigating, we realized that the checks had been signed and cashed while I was away.

In an instant, my heart dropped into my stomach. I knew exactly who had signed those checks, and it wasn't me. While I was away, I'd given my keys to my son, John Jr. I'd trusted him fully and completely to handle any issues that arose in my absence. Though I had some surplus checks in an unlocked cabinet in my office, I hadn't thought to lock it because John would be the only one with access to my locked office anyway.

I didn't know how to process what I'd just found out. Prior to that day, I'd never, under any circumstances, believe that my son would do something like this to me. I struggled to speak; to even wrap my mind around what he'd done. But the truth was staring me right in the face. My signature had been forged on checks that had been cashed while I was more than 150 miles away. I felt a sense of guilt, like I'd somehow failed as a father.

I closed my eyes, hoping that when I reopened them, I'd find myself in bed, and this would've all been some sort of cruel nightmare. Instead, I opened them to find the bookkeeper still staring at me, waiting for me to tell her what to do.

"Okay," I said, shaking my head. "We're going to have to take this to the board." The bookkeeper did her own investigation, looking back over the past six months to see if anything similar had happened before. Eventually, she was able to isolate the incident to that small window in time when I was out of town, confirming her suspicion that I had nothing to do with it.

Once I had enough information on what had occurred, I contacted Chair Armand to inform her of the details. She expressed her concerns about the matter and extended apologies to me for this awful act committed by my son. She also informed me that she had no definitive date when I could expect her to return, and thus resigned.

I later informed board member Michael Martin about what had transpired, as well as my conversation with the chair. He and I discussed the matter fully and decided to have a conversation with Herb Ames about assuming the role as interim chair. We fully briefed Herb on the matter, and he was willing to assume the role if amenable to the board.

At the time, the chamber owed me nearly $33,000 in deferred payments for my salary. I proposed that they repay the chamber out of the cash that was owed to me, and asked that they not prosecute John Jr.

Members of the board (me excluded, of course) met with John Jr. to get his account of what transpired with the stolen checks. After that, the board met to vote on the recommendation discussed between Michael, Herb, and I about how the chamber would be reimbursed for its loss.

When it came to vote, everyone agreed, except for one member, Zach Chester. Zach was also a council member for the City of Trenton. Not only did he abstain from voting, but he also resigned from the board in protest of the decision. Either way, I was grateful for how things had turned out. More than anything, I was grateful that my son would be spared from any legal ramifications.

This season of my life was awfully painful. I was struggling with feelings of inadequacy both as a father, and as president of this beloved organization. Though other Black organizations had similar problems with money, I never wanted ours to be one of them. Unfortunately, the organization that I led was now amongst that list.

Unfortunately, this whole incident coincided with our decision to bring Herb Ames on as chairman of the organization. At first, he seemed sympathetic, but before long, he started to convey some doubt about my lack of involvement. He seemed skeptical that I didn't have something to do with it; a suspicion I found both ridiculous and insulting.

Not long after, information was leaked and even folks outside of MTAACC had heard about what happened. However, as often happens in situations like this, they seemed to have a different version of the story. According to them, I was accused of siphoning funds from the chamber.

One afternoon, I was walking by the post office when I ran into a friend, a man named Juan Martinez.

"John," Juan said, looking very concerned. "Herb told me some terrible things, man. He says you were taking money from the chamber, and that you were using company credit cards? Is it true?"

I could barely believe what I was hearing. The chamber didn't even have a credit card. I thought Herb and I had moved past our personal differences and had landed where, even if we didn't necessarily like each other, we at least respected one another. But here he was, going around sullying my name. I was fuming with rage.

"Come on, Juan, what do you think, man? Of course it's not true!" I could barely keep myself from screaming. After that, my personal and professional relationship with Herb went completely left.

Herb knew that I was getting ready to launch a statewide chamber. I was operating out of the MTAACC space for some time, readying my plans while keeping a watchful eye on how MTAACC was progressing. Part of the larger plan was to have the state's three regional chambers – Trenton, Atlantic City and Northern New Jersey (which I'd helped found a few years earlier) – become divisions under the new statewide umbrella.

Before the entire fiasco bursted forward, Herb told me that he wanted to be the chair of the statewide chamber. I told him that it wasn't possible as there was already someone else lined up to occupy the role. Apparently, that refusal had set him on a new course, one with the ultimate goal of destroying me.

Not only had he been spreading rumors about me, Herb was also actively trying to sabotage my plans. One day, I went to my office only to discover that my computer had been destroyed. I didn't need proof – I already knew exactly who was responsible. The computer held all of the plans I'd been making for a statewide Chamber of Commerce. All the data, my years of planning – gone. I confronted him, but of course he denied having any involvement. Even while saying the words, he could barely conceal the smug look on his face.

I went back to my office to try to retrieve any of the information I'd lost, but my efforts were futile. As I sat there at my desk, clicking away to no avail, I felt a red-hot rage rise within me. I'd invited Herb into MTAACC. I'd offered him the position of chair which effectively brought him into the fold of the organization, and I'd blamed myself for everything that had happened since that very moment. If you see a snake in the grass, you'd better kill him right then and there. If you let him live, you bet your ass he'll be back to bite you.

Chapter 9

Troubled Waters

They say that when one door closes, another one opens. At least in some segments of my life, I found that to be true. When I officially walked away from the Metropolitan Trenton African American Chamber of Commerce, that door closed firmly behind me. In fact, after I left, the chamber eventually dissolved as well.

The organization had owed me around $30,000 in backpay, after I resigned. I was willing to work with them, despite the bad blood between Herb Ames and me while they came up with a reasonable plan that would allow them to keep serving the community while paying me back; a decision we all agreed on. But instead of finding an amicable solution, the people in charge decided it would be better to shut down the whole operation. It felt like a bitter response, but I had too many other things to focus on, so I didn't fixate on it.

At around the same time, in 2007, I officially founded the African American Chamber of Commerce of New Jersey (AACCNJ) with a small, trusted group of people, most of whom were just volunteers. We didn't have a lot of money at this point, but it was enough to rent a small 700 square-foot office space for us to work out of. We started the venture with exactly $14,000. While it was tighter than any of us would've liked, we made it work as much as possible. These were the 'lean years', as we liked to call them. I was hungry for growth, and ready for our organization to make some real, meaningful change across the state. Though we all shared in this vision, we also knew it wasn't something that could happen quickly. It required slow, steady, and consistent movement. As our footprint increased, so too would our impact. We just needed a bit of patience and grit.

There were times when we organized meetings we couldn't feasibly hold in the office, as the space was far too small to accommodate the number or status of our guests. Sometimes, we'd hold meetings at a local hotel nearby that allowed us to use their conference room. We also rented out rooms at Thomas Edison State University across the street. We were doing what we had to do while I attempted to get my plans for the group back on track.

After my computer had been destroyed at the MTAACC offices, along with my plans for the chamber, I got straight to work reconstructing everything from memory. Much to my surprise, it all came back to me with little effort. Now, we were en route to building what I hoped would be the biggest Black chamber in the state.

I knew that to do that, we needed two things: a large membership base and strategic partnerships. For us to be successful, the Black community had to believe in our mission and subscribe to it. We had to get them to see that the machine we were building had the capability to connect them to resources, opportunities, and information.

Additionally, we needed corporations as well as the government (municipal and federal) to invest and collaborate with us, and to understand that their association with our organization would help them tap into our vast network of innovative and talented individuals. There was immense value in what we had to offer, we just had to get them to believe that, too.

Not long after we got on our feet, AACCNJ held a gala that was attended by a few hundred people. Catherine Starghill, a Deputy Commissioner from the New Jersey Department of Labor, was one of the successful and well-connected individuals in attendance. She was so impressed with the event and what our organization had been able to pull off that she wanted to help us grow and expand our impact even further. At the time, the New Jersey Department of Labor was launching a new initiative called the Talent Network which connected job seekers with employers in several industries and offered lucrative grants to non-profit organizations and industry associations. To be eligible, you had to fall into one of the industry sectors within their purview. Because of my own background in banking, and AACCNJ's pursuit for economic empowerment for Black people, we fell comfortably into the financial services sector.

Catherine encouraged us to apply, and even though we weren't initially selected to be the prime contractor (which came with a hefty $250,000 grant), we still received many other important and helpful opportunities. We got access to resources, a huge boost to our credibility, and much more exposure for the work we were doing.

The following year, when the grant was up for renewal, Catherine felt confident that if AACCNJ applied, we'd get the prime contract. I was a little hesitant at first, not nearly as sure or secure as Catherine. But, buoyed by her resolve and insistence, we gathered all of the required documents, constructed a proposal, and submitted our application. Within no time, Catherine called to report that she had some news.

I steadied my breath as she spoke, clearly stretching the conversation to increase the suspense.

"Come on now, Catherine," I laughed nervously, interrupting her attempt at small talk. "What's the news?" She laughed, and then quickly fell silent.

"John," she said, pausing for what felt like forever, my name lingering in the silence. "You got it! The chamber got the grant!" I shouted with joy, excitedly relaying the good news to the rest of the team, who were all staring at me expectantly. This was a huge win for us. With the boost of cash, and the implied vote of confidence in our mission, we now possessed the ability to truly expand our capacity.

Our visibility increased almost overnight. The state was pushing the Talent Network's agenda forward, and now we were an important part of it. As a result, we visited financial institutions regularly, and connected people within our networks to greater access to jobs and opportunities.

We were on an upward trajectory, and growing at a pace that both excited and terrified me. With our new-found credibility, our confidence increased, too. We began reaching out to corporations to inquire about potential collaborations while recommending our members and their companies for contracts. Things moved quickly.

I knew I wanted to work with some big, well-known corporations, and had determined that partnerships like those would give AACCNJ even more pull and legitimacy in the marketplace. Thanks to our contract with the Talent Network, we were already building important connections with government agencies, and with our name next to these corporate giants, it would only propel us further.

When I reached out to Linda Johnson, the lead specialist in talent acquisition at PSE&G (one of the largest utility companies in New Jersey), she gave us a $20,000 training grant.

Beverly Jennings, the head of Global Supplier Diversity and Inclusion at Johnson & Johnson, shared demographic information from the company about Black spending. Together, and with this data, Beverly and I co-wrote an article about the financial benefits and rewards of increased diversity. These collaborations were solidifying AACCNJ as a major player, and were setting us up for even more growth.

I should mention an important observation I had back then, which has only been clarified and solidified further with time — Black women have been responsible for so much of the success I've achieved, both personally and professionally in my life. It is due to their continuous and genuine support of my mission that I've been able to get as far as I've gotten with my work. And it's not just me. AACCNJ would almost certainly not be what it is today if it weren't for their contributions. Catherine Starghill is a Black woman. Linda Johnson, Beverly Jennings, Jacqueline Baptiste (who is my right-hand woman at the chamber), and the list goes on. These women have all stuck out their necks for me and for AACCNJ over the years, and have become my guardian angels in life and work.

I met folks around this time, people who had important roles within major corporations, who all took the time to listen to me, and truly hear what I had to say. They were genuinely interested in learning more about what it was like for a small business owner trying to make it, and what it was like for minority business owners, too. Being a spokesman and an advocate for these groups was no easy feat, but I quickly learned to approach those conversations with empathy. It taught me to meet people where they were, not where I wanted them to be.

As AACCNJ's star continued to rise, we were making significant strides, and found ourselves growing at an exponential rate. But at the same time, I was also beginning to recognize that some things had started to wind down in my personal life. Specifically, my marriage. Over the years, Lennice and I had been tested, and our bond put through the ringer. We'd experienced so many financial hardships, losses, and career changes, and each challenge left us weathered and beaten.

There was a time years earlier, in 2000, when the doubts about my marriage had weighed on me so heavily, I seriously contemplated leaving my family. But when I'd return home at the end of a long day at work, I'd see my boys' faces as they excitedly told me all about their days, completely ignorant to the plan formulating in my mind. In those moments, I'd dissolve the desire to leave, if only temporarily. As I watched Lennice patiently setting the table, the calm and serene look on her face as our sons laughed and gathered around her, I couldn't bear to lose the beautiful life we'd built together.

But by 2009, it was almost a decade later, and I was still grappling with so many of those same doubts and uncertainties about whether we truly wanted the same things. I'd been mentally and emotionally checked out of my marriage for the last few years; far more focused on building out these Black chambers than on mending the massive rift that had formed between Lennice and me. It wasn't that I didn't want to fix things, I just reached a dead-end within myself.

For years, it felt like every path I wanted to pursue required me to first overcome the hurdle of Lennice's hesitations. When I first wanted to start my own trucking company, she had been entirely against it. When I wanted to bring someone in to help after I returned to the bank, per her insistence, she shot that down. When I quit the bank a second time to focus on Harmon Transfer Corp., she was deeply unhappy. When I started MTAACC, she didn't believe anything would come of it. And when I founded AACCNJ, she still wasn't on board.

I understood her reluctance in most of those scenarios. I knew that I was asking her to follow me down uncertain paths; to risk our stability for the sake of my passions. Even when I failed, I still felt confident that things would right themselves, that I'd find my footing once again, and that our family would thrive. I'm an eternal optimist. I believed then, just as I do now, that things will work out.

Lennice didn't share that perspective; she was far more pragmatic. It's true that we faced some hardships due to my career shifts, but the kids were always happy and well-dressed. We always had a roof over our heads and a hot meal on the table. I felt the sacrifices we had to make were worth it, and were all leading to a larger and more fulfilling payout for us all. For one thing, if I'd stayed at the bank instead of going out on my own all of those years ago, I don't think I would've been able to nurture my relationships with my kids as much as I had. I wouldn't have had the time to coach their sports teams or attend their games. It's possible we would've had more money, lived a more stable and luxurious lifestyle, but I wouldn't have been around as much.

Either way, the years of arguments and clashing perspectives on how we should live had taken its toll. I had no more fight in me. I felt, deep in my core, that we just didn't want the same things, any maybe never did.

A few years earlier, in 2007, New Jersey enacted into law a statute that allowed for no-fault divorce. Couples could now file for divorce based on irrevocable differences. Once the thought entered my mind, there was no going back. The process was simple, all I had to do was fill out some paperwork, and then get Lennice to sign on the dotted line. I picked up the divorce kit for $4.99, and went through the pages, completing all of the sections that required my signature. When I was finished, I placed the pages on the bed for Lennice and left the house. I felt anxious as hell, unsure of how she'd respond. We'd spoken about divorce plenty of times before, always falling just short of going through with it. But now, I'd done it and I hadn't even spoken with her about it. I suppose some part of me knew that she wouldn't be in agreement, and I didn't want to have that conversation again. I didn't want to get trapped in a back and forth discussion that would inevitably end with me backing down. I'd already made up my mind.

When I got home later that evening, Lennice was in the kitchen. As soon as our eyes met, I knew that she'd seen the paperwork. Her face looked pained, and like she'd been crying. I wasn't divorcing Lennice due to a lack of feelings; I'd always have so much love for her. Seeing her hurting pulled at my heart. It made me want to wrap my arms around her. I wanted to protect her, to stifle whatever was causing her to suffer, even if that something was me.

I gulped hard, swallowing the tentacles of uncertainty that were latching onto my throat. This time, I had to stand my ground. Longevity isn't a good enough reason to stay in a marriage, and we were doing each other a disservice by staying together when we were both so unhappy.

Later, when we were out of earshot of the boys, in the cold and cavernous silence of our bedroom, we finally got a chance to talk.

"Why, John?" Lennice asked, the desperation in her voice striking me right in the heart. I exhaled, slowly lowering myself onto the bed.

"We've talked about this, Len," I said, gesturing for her to sit next to me. She stayed standing, her arms crossed in front of her. "We've discussed it. And I just reached my breaking point. This is what I want to do. I think this is what's best for the both of us."

She stared at me, her large brown eyes searching mine for answers she clearly felt she wasn't getting from my words. We stayed like that for a few moments, both of us watching each other as the silence grew sharper and more potent with every passing second. Finally, Lennice broke eye contact.

"Well," she said, pacing the room now, "if that's what you want to do." She shot me one last look, shrugged, and walked out.

At the time, both Joshua and Justin were away at college, so only John Jr. was living with us. We waited until our family was all under the same roof a few weeks later to break the news. As Lennice and I sat next to each other on the loveseat, we called the guys to come join us. John Jr., Josh, and Justin threw themselves onto the various couches and sofas, laughing and joking around.

"What's up, Dad?" Josh said, staring at me expectantly. My heart broke as I looked at my kids, at how grown each of them had become. Part of the reason I'd waited so long to do this was because I didn't want to interrupt their childhoods. But now, as I watched their long-limbed bodies sprawled out before me, I realized my boys were barely boys anymore; they were men. I shook off the nostalgia, exhaled, and steadied myself.

"Listen guys, your mother and I have something really important to tell you," I said, slapping my hands on my knees. "This isn't easy to say. And I want you to know that we love you all, so much. But.. Umm.. We're.."

"We're getting divorced," Lennice interrupted me, her voice firm and steady. Their jaws all dropped in sync, the shock setting into their faces as the meaning of the words sunk in. They looked confused, as if we'd spoken to them in a foreign language.

"What?" Justin said, breaking the silence. "What do you mean? How? *Why*? You guys don't even fight. I've never seen you fight." It was true, over the years, Lennice and I had made every effort to keep our arguments away from the kids. Instead, we always fought quietly, and in the privacy of our room. We shielded the boys from our dysfunction to protect them, but perhaps, in an unexpected way, it just ended up creating an even more jarring conclusion. In their minds, Lennice and I were happier than ever. It was a plot-twist they never could have imagined.

They weren't the only ones surprised. As we slowly began breaking the news to our families and friends, everyone seemed to have a similar reaction. Disbelief. Incredulity. We'd always seemed so happy together, they all said. No one could have predicted this.

After announcing the divorce, Lennice and I tried, as much as possible, to maintain a sense of normalcy in the home. We continued with many of our long-held traditions. I was still the boys' basketball coach, and we both still attended all of their games. We still had pizza and chicken wings every Friday night. I was still their dad, and Lennice was still their mom; a reality that would never change, even if we stopped being husband and wife.

The only problem was that, at least for the first few months, Lennice refused to engage with the paperwork, hemming and hawing for as long as she could. Even though we'd notified everyone else in our lives about the end of our relationship, Lennice still seemed unwilling to move things forward — to make the divorce real.

There was a sunset period on this stage of the process though, and if she didn't take action, eventually, I'd be able to get a default in my favor. I'd hoped we could get the whole divorce settled without lawyers so we'd be able to work together on splitting our assets, and deciding on who got what. But Lennice had other plans in mind. Before the sunset period expired, she lawyered up. Whatever idea I had about an amicable divorce quickly disappeared. For the next year, we fought at nearly every step of the process. If our boys weren't legally adults, we probably would've fought over their custody, too.

A year after I left the paperwork on the bed, on June 6, 2010, Lennice and I were finally divorced. Our separation was officially final, at least in the legal sense. But we still had the house to deal with. Given that the housing market was depressed, which placed our property value under water, we made an agreement to put it on the market 18 months after our divorce was finalized. We did so with the hopes that by then, things would've improved. During that period, however, I continued to make timely payments on the mortgage.

After Lennice moved out of the house, I lived there alone for a while. Josh had relocated to New Orleans for a job, and Justin was living in Miami. John Jr. had moved to Pennsylvania with his girlfriend. I was still trying to figure out my life as I wrestled with feelings of uncertainty and loneliness. I hadn't been alone for more than 20 years. I was used to sleeping next to Lennice, and to having a steady stream of bodies come into and out of the house. But now, there was just stillness and silence.

In 2015, I had to deed my house back to the bank. I'd been trying, futilely, for the past few years to get Lennice to sign an agreement, granting full ownership of the house and its remaining debt solely to my name. For reasons that have never made any sense to me, she refused. She hadn't lived there for years, and I was the only one who'd ever made any payments on the mortgage. I'd been going through negotiations with the bank for years, and after the divorce, I applied for a hardship modification with my bank, which they approved. This meant that for a year, I made reduced payments on the mortgage until I was more stable. After that year was up, they agreed to extend the modification another six months. By this point, Lennice and I had been divorced for 18 months, which meant we should've been getting the house ready to sell. But with a collapsed housing market, and the aftermath of a financial crisis still hot in the air, that became nearly impossible.

The bank proposed a different offer. Since I'd had a spotless record of making my payments on the house up until that point, they were willing to restructure the loan terms so that I could become the sole owner of the house, and continue making payments. If Lennice agreed to deed the house back to me, I'd become the sole owner of both the house and the debt; a responsibility I was willing to absorb to honor my commitment to the bank. Lennice and I had been divorced for nearly two years by now, and she'd been out of the house for almost as long. In my mind, it shouldn't have mattered to her.

We remained in that limbo — me trying to convince Lennice to sign the house over to me, Lennice refusing without giving me a real reason why — for a

while. By 2015, the jig was up. The bank was seeking to foreclose on the house, and I, in turn, negotiated a deed in lieu without a deficiency judgment. This meant I had to find somewhere else to live.

The bank graciously offered me some money to help with the transition expenses. I packed up all of my belongings into boxes and suitcases and moved them to a storage facility not too far away. Then, I moved into my niece's basement where I attempted to figure out my next steps.

The past few years of my life had done a huge number on me. I was the president of one of the most successful Black chambers in the country, and now I was sleeping on an air mattress in my niece's basement, alone. It wasn't how I pictured I'd be living when I was 55. Still, despite the darkness of my current circumstances, my faith never faltered. As they say, great testimonies are a result of great tests.

I was struggling, sure. But that struggle wouldn't last forever. It couldn't. And I knew, deep in my soul, that I was heading down the right path. The path most aligned with my purpose. I'd made many mistakes in my life, up until this point. I'd failed more times than I could even keep track of. But, I'd always stayed true to myself, and that had to matter for something.

Not too long after I'd moved into my niece's house, I remember attending church one Sunday morning when the pastor was giving a sermon about coping during difficult times in life.

"If you're connected to a solid foundation, you have something to lean on in tough times, something to shield you from unforeseen dangers," he preached from his pulpit. "That foundation is your faith, it's your scriptures. It's God." I felt like he was speaking directly to me.

"God will get you through the tough times," he said, looking in my direction. If I had any hesitations about the direction I was going in, they dissipated in that instant. I felt more confident than ever that I was going exactly where I was meant to go.

Chapter 10

The Devil Is in the Details

The older I've gotten, the more I've realized that life is just a series of wins and losses, oscillating back and forth between each other endlessly. The good times are usually followed by challenging ones, and the bad ones don't last forever. After years of challenges – personally, professionally, and financially – the success of the African American Chamber of Commerce of New Jersey was like a salve for my soul.

Our organization received a level of credibility and respect that opened many doors, and allowed our work to make a greater impact across the state. We were even able to forge a working relationship with Governor Chris Christie, a connection that created opportunities we may not have had otherwise. I also began to reach out to banks and corporations to introduce our organization and build what we hoped to be lasting relationships.

Our group was still in that small, 700 square-foot office building, and even though there were only a handful of us at the time, we all squished together in that shoebox, forced to be more intimate than any of us would've liked. After a few months there, I broached the topic of finding a new office building with the group. In fact, I already had the perfect place in mind: 379 West State Street. The building had gone into mild disrepair after its owner, a local dentist, and his family had died tragically in a plane crash. As a result, his estate had been trying to sell the property for some time, with little luck.

Fortunately for me, the property was once used for parking by employees of the State of New Jersey. Since their lease had been terminated by the state, it meant that the value of the property had diminished significantly. The property had previously been listed for over one million dollars, but now the estate lacked the revenue to offset the expenses of the property. I was contacted by the realtor who informed me that the property was now available for a mere $125,000. I was shocked and surprised all at the same time.

I shared the news with the group, excitedly. They all looked at me sideways, reminding me that even though we were growing at a steady pace, we were still in our infancy, and our bank balance reflected that. To put it softly, we didn't have the money. But I was unfazed. I knew that if we played our cards and our connections right, we could get the cash.

To see my plan through, I wrote a letter to Kevin Cummins, the chairman and CEO of Investors Bank, a local Trenton-based institution. In it, I shared with him AACCNJ's desire to purchase the building at 379 West

State Street – and requested their help. I explained what the building would do to elevate our group's awareness, and how it would help us to achieve our goals. I told him that the bank's help would become a part of their legacy in Trenton; their support of the Black community and Black businesses would be written into history books.

A few weeks later, he called my office and asked me to come by the bank for a meeting. When I arrived, I was met by Kevin, the president of the bank, Domenick Cama, and a few other senior executives. After taking some time to discuss the chamber's goals, and how the new building would bring them to fruition, they thanked me for coming, and promised to be in touch. I didn't know what to think, and to be honest, I didn't feel very hopeful. I'd been in these situations before, pouring out a heartfelt pitch to a group of people with the power to make a huge difference in my life, only to be left in the dust. Still, I tried not to lose hope entirely. A few weeks later, John Nietzel, the Senior Vice President of Investors Bank called me to give me an update.

"Well John, we have an offer for you," he said. I lifted my eyebrow, curiously.

"I'm listening," I said, holding the phone receiver to my ear with my shoulder. He went on to explain that the bank would offer our group a $200,000 grant, as well as a $50,000 line of credit. I nearly dropped the phone to the ground, fumbling to pick it up.

"You there, John?" Kevin laughed into the phone.

"I'm here, man. I'm here," I laughed back. I thanked him, and told him how appreciative the chamber was for the bank's help. When I shared the news with the rest of the group, they were all ecstatic.

Following the acquisition of 379 West State Street, I met with several of our members who had construction businesses. The goal was to assemble a team to renovate the building. I made it clear to each of them that the building would be a resource for our members, and would contribute greatly to our creditability and mission, therefore, they should keep that in mind when submitting their cost estimates.

The building was completely renovated and ready for occupancy in less than a year. We now had, thanks to Investors Bank, a 5,500 square-foot, three-story building, with a parking lot that could accommodate over 100 cars. The building ultimately cost us $130,000. The ribbon cutting ceremony for our new headquarters was attended by representatives from the governor's office, and the mayor of the City of Trenton. Representatives from Investors Bank, various corporations, along with our members and other community stakeholders were also there, too. This was a major accomplishment for the AACCNJ, and it was being celebrated by all.

After the day-long celebration, my team and I continued to make even more progress. We began to fine-tune our internal and external strategies, focusing on how to build out more awareness to increase our value proposition on New Jersey's economy. Importantly, we thought about our members and what they'd gain from joining. How could we connect more Black businesses to greater opportunities and community programming? How could we ensure that when the government and corporations had contracts available, Black business owners were front and center? Through our tireless effort, we'd made some very important strides, and within a few years, we'd managed to become one of the most successful Black chambers in the country.

When AACCNJ was up and running, out of the development stages and deep into the execution phase, I began thinking of how to expand our influence even further. New York, which is a huge and important stomping ground for Black folks and businesses, didn't have a chamber. I thought that perhaps, with the support and encouragement of the National Black Chamber, we could build one. I imagined the partnerships and collaborations we could forge with New York and New Jersey working together.

In 2010, I started researching statistics about New York. There was a larger Black population there than in New Jersey, and the number of Black businesses was somewhere around 200,000, in comparison to

New Jersey who had 88,000 at the time. When you factored in population sizes, proportionally, we were around the same. Additionally, when it came to the challenges our communities faced in our respective states, they were also very similar.

When I was in the preparation stages, getting my forms and proposals together to begin the process of incorporating the New York chamber, I met a woman named Charlotte Hitchcock who worked as an attorney for the state of New Jersey. We began casually talking, and I shared my plan with her. She seemed genuinely interested, and expressed her interest in getting involved. Of course, I was happy for any help I could get. We agreed to stay in touch, and over the next few weeks, as we deepened our relationship and got to know each other better, she offered to take care of preparing the incorporation and federal tax status documents for a fee.

At that point, we had a small, core group of people. There was my friend Jay Alexander, who was on the board of the National Black Chamber (NBCC) with me, and who'd brought a few business leaders he'd known from New York into the fold. Some New Jersey members got involved, as well, and once we finished filling out all of the incorporation documents, I sent them over to Charlotte to file.

As the months passed, I started to get impatient. I'd incorporated many companies before and knew it didn't usually take this long. I contacted the State of

New York to inquire on our application. Much to my surprise, the guy on the other end of the line told me that it had been withdrawn.

"Withdrawn?" I shouted into the phone. "How? I didn't withdraw it. How did that happen?" I was utterly confused. The man told me that it must have been withdrawn by the same person who filed it. That would've been Charlotte. I immediately called her to ask why she'd done something like that. After not receiving a straight or satisfactory answer, I told her I'd refile it myself.

She apologized profusely and assured me that if I filed, she'd do her best to push it along to make sure it was completed quickly. But just like the first time around, I watched the clock, and the process was still going around the Mulberry bush; a slow and meandering process. I reached out to the state once again for an update, and like the time before, they informed me that it had been withdrawn...again. I didn't need to wonder who had done it this time.

I was *hot,* and fuming with anger.

I didn't understand why she was doing this. I'd paid her for filing the first time, but the second time, she had nothing to do with it. For reasons I never understood or learned, Charlotte was trying to sabotage our efforts. Whatever her reasoning, which I didn't even care to know, I had to get her to stop.

I wrote a letter to her, describing my annoyance and confusion at her doing such a thing.

"I'm resubmitting the application," I wrote, "and if it gets withdrawn one more time, I'll have no choice but to tell Governor Christie." I knew that would do the trick; Charlotte was an officer of the court in New Jersey, and if she was caught pulling moves to intentionally mess with our efforts to uplift the Black community, she'd have hell to pay. It was a scathing reminder that not everyone was on our side. I refiled, and within no time, we were registered and good to go.

It was also around this time that I was deepening my connection to the National Black Chamber of Commerce, and particularly to its founders, Kay DeBow Alford and Harry Alford. They'd taught me about the Black diaspora, about the communities outside of the U.S., and the influence they were having in their endeavors. The National Black Chamber even had an entire division focused on forging international relationships with other nations. Harry and Kay encouraged me to get more involved on that front, and in 2002, I embarked on my first trip with them to Ghana.

From the moment I stepped foot off the plane, and placed my feet firmly on the ground, something felt different. I couldn't quite explain it, but there was an aching in my chest; the feeling of a loop closing. In a way, it felt like I had just come home.

As we were taken around throughout the country, I was struck by the pride and dignity of the people. Everywhere I looked, the women walked with their heads held high, regardless of their status. I felt myself being pulled to learn more about the history of Ghana, and of myself, too. Everywhere I looked, I saw Black people in charge. Black folks in power. They were the government, the business owners, the lawyers, doctors – everything. Of course, I'd known this before coming to Ghana, but seeing it with my own two eyes was surreal. I was used to fighting for my place, but here, it seemed as though Black people belonged everywhere.

After getting a tour of the stock exchange and commerce departments, we visited Cape Coast Castle in the south of Ghana, which was essentially a depot that held enslaved people kidnapped from across Africa between the 16th and 19th centuries. Brutally taken from their homes, they were locked in the dungeons at Cape Coast Castle (or one of the 40 others) before being loaded onto ships to cross the Atlantic Ocean. As we walked through the massive structure, the tour guide described the atrocities that had taken place within its walls.

When we reached the 'Door of No Return', I couldn't stop thinking about one sobering fact: this had been their final stop before being shipped off and distributed to different countries. My ancestors stood there, in front of the angry expanse of sea, before being cast off to a foreign land that they knew nothing about. Separated from their culture, language, and entire way of life, they were forced into lives of brutality and servitude. I had to continuously gulp back the lump that was forming in my throat, leaving me on the verge of tears.

But it wasn't only sadness I was grappling with. I was pissed off, and I couldn't help but to level my anger at a very specific target: white folks. I was angry about how my people were treated centuries after the slave trade had officially ended.

It was a lot to unpack. But it also helped define my purpose even more when I returned home. I became more intentional about articulating our value proposition, and our contributions to society. I become far more vocal about reminding people – politicians, in particular – that there was a great debt owed to Black people. The trip, in so many ways, had changed my life.

After Ghana, I was hooked. I wanted to be more involved with our international efforts, to be part of the work we were doing to create connections with other nations, and to learn more about what Black folks were doing outside of the U.S.

In 2003, Harry invited chamber presidents from Jamaica to Washington in the hopes that we might be able to start a sister-city relationship with one of the chambers in the Caribbean country.

When they arrived, Harry took them on a full tour of Washington, and explained the history of the National Black Chamber. They visited Congress, and were even able to meet a few legislators. Afterwards, Harry brought them to New Jersey where we invited them into our building for a day spent learning more about each other.

Not long after their trip, we were invited to visit Jamaica. We stayed at a resort in Negril that was owned by an African American woman named Gail Jackson. It was a stunning space, built right on the golden sandy shores of the Caribbean Sea. She and her husband, a Jamaican man who owned an ice business, welcomed us as though we were long lost family members. But it wasn't just the hospitality that made Jamaica feel so special. I learned that many of their chambers had been around for more than 100 years. The National Black Chamber at home wasn't even two decades old at this point. Of course, we had an oppressive and devastating history that had prevented our ancestors from being able to advocate for us, but it revealed to me just how much farther we had to go, and how much more we had to learn.

While we were there, we tried our best to create a sense of connectivity, and to match some of our businesses with theirs to see how we could help each other out, and pull each other up. Unfortunately, the relationship didn't last for too long, as our cultural differences, especially regarding time, infringed on our ability to get anything done.

After Jamaica, we visited Colombia, where we set up a Colombian African Chamber of Commerce. It was very well-received, with over 300 people showing up to the inaugural event. Later, we traveled to Cuba, Costa Rica, and a few other countries, as well.

I loved learning about other cultures, and seeing the way Black culture existed in these places. But the most important aspect of the work we were doing was the lessons I brought home. Afterall, the entire point of going on these trips was to learn skills and strategies on how to advocate more effectively for my people in the U.S. I was proud of all that the chamber had been able to accomplish, but there was one project in particular that made me feel as though all of my hard work was truly having an impact.

By 2012, I'd been working with Black businesses for more than a decade. One of AACCNJ's major functions was to help Black business owners land public contracts, which were often lucrative, life-changing opportunities. Throughout the years, there was one sticking point that prevented many of these more than qualified companies from landing the jobs: bonds. The state, county, and municipal governments could only hire bonded contractors. To secure the job, companies needed to provide a bond, which essentially an insurance instrument that would protect the hiring company in case the one being contracted defaulted on getting the job done. In the event that this occurred, they would be able to use that bond to hire someone else. Since many small businesses didn't have a lot of liquid assets, they couldn't afford this extra requirement, thus excluding them from applying for these jobs.

Anytime I listened to a politician celebrate some new project, and all of the job opportunities it would create, I found myself getting more and more frustrated. They weren't wrong for their excitement, but the devil was in the details: the opportunities were reserved for those who could afford them. I'd been a small business owner myself so I knew the challenges intimately. I also knew how defeating it could be to have opportunities for growth right in front of you, but ones you were unable to pursue.

This knowledge, and the frustration it created, led me on a year's long quest to create change. I knew that if we could at least establish some sort of program to help Black businesses with the bonding process, it would significantly transform the playing field.

I spoke with politicians and legislators on the state, municipal, and county levels, explaining my grievances to them. They agreed that something needed to be done, but no one seemed to have any solutions. As I tried to figure out how to navigate this process, I met a man named David Cayemitte, an insurance broker and bonding agent instrumental in getting a similar program established in New York.

He'd been down this sometimes-infuriating path before, so he helped guide me through.

After several years of meetings, and even more broken promises, I was finally able to convince a group of Republican Legislators from New Jersey that establishing a bonding readiness program would be a significant step in positioning small businesses to compete for public contracts in our state. Republican Senator Pennacchio was willing to sponsor the bill, but asked me to identify a Democrat to co-sponsor it. I rifled through my contacts, and that's when I came across the perfect person: Senator Rice. When I called him up to ask for his support, he eagerly agreed.

After that, the bill was passed unanimously, and signed into law in 2016 by Governor Chris Christie. The moment became even more meaningful when Governor Christie held the bill signing in the conference room at the AACCNJ. He brought the press along with him, and it was a major accomplishment for our chamber.

Soon after, the Small Business Bonding Readiness Assistance Program came into effect. It included an 8-week course where the entrepreneurs were able to take classes, workshops, and counseling sessions to prepare.

Our success with the bonding program, as well as the recognition I was beginning to receive – from the national chamber and other organizations around the state – bolstered my confidence, and made me want to share our successes with the other chambers.

Each time AACCNJ attended National Black Chamber conferences, and other meetings where I had an opportunity to tell our story, I constantly spoke, at length, about all the great things our organization was doing in New Jersey. Although we were still in our infancy compared to other chambers, we'd developed a track record of success. We'd coalesced an excellent working relationship with the governor, we had a business model that differed from some of the other chambers, and we had a strategy that we'd come up with all on our own. I was proud of us, but I also wanted to inspire other groups to try coloring outside the lines, too.

One year around, I was invited to the U.S. Hispanic Chamber of Commerce's annual conference. I'd known for some time that their organization was extremely successful as they'd managed to gain access to rooms and tables that I wanted our groups to be at, too. When I arrived at the conference, however, I quickly realized that I'd somehow underestimated just how big their influence was. They had hundreds, if not thousands of people in attendance, and major corporate sponsors.

Toyota, Cadillac, Well Fargo – the names were huge. As I walked around, taking stock of the impressive event, I couldn't help but compare it to the National

Black Chamber's annual conference. It went without saying; ours paled in comparison.

During our stay, myself and another board member named Arnold Baker set up a meeting with Javier Palomarez, the CEO of the Hispanic chamber. He was an impressive, nationally respected figure, and I felt like there was a lot I could learn from him. More importantly, I felt as though our organizations had the ability to make even bigger strides for our communities if we joined forces. Javier, it seemed, had something similar in mind.

"Listen John, neither of us are really getting what we deserve from these political parties," he said, leaning back in his chair. "If we worked together, we could get so much more done." I instantly agreed. We discussed a strategy to unify, and, at the end, Javier said he was in.

"This sounds great," Javier said, shaking my hand. "Run it by Harry and get back to me." Arnold and I were over the moon. We felt like we'd just secured a huge win for the chamber, and I assumed Harry and the other board members would agree.

I approached Harry with the news shortly after, excitedly relaying Javier's eagerness to come together. Much to my surprise, Harry didn't seem to mirror my enthusiasm. His face tightened as a sour expression spread across his face.

"Javier knows where I'm at. We're both in Washington," he said, a sharpness in his voice. "He should reach out to me himself." I didn't know what to say or how to respond, so I stood there processing his reaction. As an organization, we'd discussed these kinds of strategic partnerships before. And now, the ability to pursue one was right in front of us, and Harry was refusing to follow up. I didn't understand his inaction, but it wasn't my place to do anything about it. Harry was the president of the National Black Chamber, and I was just a board member at the time.

I returned to New Jersey, and to the AACCNJ, ready to get back to work serving my community. A few days later, Harry called me at the office and told me that he had me on speaker phone. With him were Chuck DeBow, the vice president; Kenny DeBow, a co-founder; Claude Macdougall, a board member; and Anthony Robinson, a board member and attorney with the Minority Black Business Defense League. I sat at my desk, fidgeting with a pen, nervous about why they were all calling me. But Harry didn't leave me much time to wonder. "You're probably wondering what this is about," he said, as if reading my mind. "Well John, some people are questioning your loyalty, and if you're really on board with the chamber." I dropped my pen, dumbfounded. Questioning my *loyalty*? Where was this even coming from?

"Harry, who are these people? And what have I ever done to have my commitment to this group put in doubt?" I tried to steady myself so I could respond with as much patience and grace as I could, but there was a smolder growing hot inside me.

"You know, John, that doesn't really matter," he responded, skirting around. Despite my professional appearance, and the way I carry myself, I'm still just a guy from North Trenton. I wasn't about to take this accusation on the chin. By this point, the smolder had grown into a flame, and I could barely contain myself.

"I have done so much to support the efforts of the National Black Chamber. I go to bat for you all every single time," I shouted, the hurt deepening with every word. "For you to question my loyalty like this, I can't believe it."

And it was true. I couldn't believe it. I worked every single day, totaling almost 100 hours a week. I saw the inside of my office more than my own house. Even though the National Black Chamber wasn't my baby in the same way that AACCNJ was, I was equally committed. I dedicated hundreds of hours, traveled anywhere they needed me to, attended conferences, meetings;— I'd done everything. I'd been challenged by people at home, in Trenton, and even within greater New Jersey, itself. But this was the first time anyone out of state had attacked my character in this way. I felt betrayed, and in a way, unsure of what to do.

Kay DeBow, Harry's wife and co-founder of the National Black Chamber, was the only one who had my back throughout the entire ordeal. Though she hadn't been there in the meeting, I later learned that she came to my defense, telling the others that they'd been wrong about me. She told them quite matter of factly that I wasn't the guy they were accusing me of being.

While I was glad for Kay's vote of confidence, I still felt saddened by how things had gone. But regardless of how the others felt about me and my intentions, I still had work to do. I knew that so many people, within my chamber and on the national front, depended on me. So I got back to work. But that knife stayed lodged in my back for some time; a subtle, aching reminder that no matter how good your intentions were, there was always someone waiting for your downfall.

Chapter 11

Unprecedented Times

When you start a new venture like the one I did with the African American Chamber of Commerce of New Jersey, growth sometimes happens in small trickles. You land a few coveted contracts, you gain some new members, and you get spatters of media attention here and there. It doesn't seem like much at first, but slowly, the droplets of success start to pile up, and the trickle turns into a deluge of wins. With enough time, the contracts get bigger, membership explodes, and the press releases become more frequent, and much more significant.

By 2019, AACCNJ was on an upward swing. That year, our annual gala was held in a ballroom at The Venetian, a luxurious venue with high ceilings and a stunning marble promenade. Our attendance was the highest it had ever been, with impressive and noteworthy names on our guest list. Throughout the year, we'd held conferences and golf tournaments, and a range of other events that attracted substantial participation. We launched a program to eradicate illiteracy in New Jersey, and another to help ex-offenders launch their own businesses to ease their transition back into society. We had contracts with the Department of Community Affairs, the Department of Labor, and the New Jersey Economic Development Authority, all which had been renewed several times over.

Even when Chris Christie's tenure as governor of New Jersey came to an end in 2017, and the Democrats took control with Phil Murphy at the helm, that didn't slow us down in the least. The new leadership was as eager and willing to work with us as their predecessors.

By the end of 2019, our revenue had crossed the $1 million mark for the first time ever. To think, when we started, we'd done so with a cool $14,000. Of that amount, $10,000 had been donated from the Northern New Jersey Black Chamber of Commerce when it had closed its doors, and now we'd crossed into seven figures. It was hard to not be excited for the future, and to set our sights on even higher heights when the stars seemed to be aligning in our favor.

As the new year kicked off, we released our 2020 calendar which contained a jam-packed schedule full of highly-anticipated social and networking events, conferences, workshops, and more. Unfortunately, none of that came into fruition, at least not in the way we'd expected.

At the top of the year, a new and mysterious illness began congesting hospitals, sending the world into a confused and terrified frenzy. COVID-19, a highly contagious disease that spread easily through airborne particles and infected surfaces, moved like wildfire across the country, and the entire world, at large. In early March, New Jersey received its first confirmed case, and within a few days, New Jersey governor Phil Murphy declared a state of emergency.

Schools and universities were closed, and students shifted to new online learning protocols. Non-essential businesses, like gyms, movie theaters, shopping malls, and casinos were forced to close, while restaurants were limited to take-out and delivery orders. Wearing a mask in any public setting became the norm, as did meticulously sanitizing your hands, door knobs, and groceries. Offices transitioned to a new work from home structure, and implemented extreme social distancing measures for staff members who had to remain on-site.

It was a strange time for everyone as we were all experiencing the stretch of unprecedented events unfolding day by day. At the AACCNJ, we had to figure things out very quickly. I couldn't quite grasp the concept of working remotely, since the very nature of our business existed through networking, face-to-face interactions, get-togethers, and in-person events. Maybe I'm just old-school, but the notion of interacting behind screens, and on conference calls just didn't jive with my soul.

Still, regardless of what I wanted, the world had changed in a fundamental way. If we wanted to stay relevant and operative, we had to make the shift, and fast. My colleague Jacqueline has two daughters, Nicole and Noelle, and bless their hearts, as they immediately swept in to help. We agreed on a hybrid work schedule – three days in office, two at home. To ensure we were abiding by the social-distancing and COVID-19 rules, we had the office retrofitted with air purifiers, and we staggered folks' work schedules to limit the number of people in the office on any given day. Since our interactions would be so limited, we had our staff members submit weekly reports to help us keep track of what everyone was doing, and how they were spending their time. Much to my surprise, productivity sky-rocketed. Our employees were getting things done at an unprecedented pace, and any concerns I'd had about the viability of remote work quickly dissipated.

As soon as we settled into our new hybrid routines, my team and I began discussing ways to continue executing on our mission, while providing value to the community. The events we'd become so well-known for before the pandemic seemed irrelevant now, as all of our members were just trying to grapple with the new reality facing us all. The truth was, misinformation about COVID-19 was spreading just as quickly as the disease, and too many people didn't know where to turn for advice or guidance. One of our board members recognized that void and suggested we try to fill it.

We got in touch with some of our healthcare partners, like Horizon, Blue Cross and Blue Shield, and Hackensack Meridian Health. Together, we began hosting daily and weekly webinars. We worked with a broad and an ever-changing roster of panelists that consisted of healthcare professionals, government officials, scientists, and researchers who covered topics ranging from what is COVID-19 and where did it come from, to addressing concerns about the vaccines and the ever-growing wave of misinformation. While the majority of press conferences and media attention was focused on the broader repercussions of the pandemic, we spoke about the rising number of cases within the Black community. Many of our attendees had chronic diseases like diabetes, high blood pressure, and heart conditions, and the pandemic added a thick layer of urgency and alarm. Black folks were already marginalized within the realm of healthcare, but with a life-threatening disease quite literally hanging in the air, they needed experts who could speak more directly to *their* experiences, *their* fears, and *their* anxieties. We provided that support, and became a source that communities all over the country could turn to for prevalent and life-saving information. Our webinars were so well-attended that media organizations like the New York Times, CNN, and USA Today were reaching out to me to discuss the success of our work.

Our webinars also helped to connect us with individuals who may not have known of us otherwise. Many Black business owners were reaching out to us, frustrated with pandemic regulations that had forced them to close. We realized that we weren't only dealing with a health crisis, but a business crisis, too. With their doors shuttered, many small businesses were being forced to close indefinitely. With no end date on the horizon, many Black business owners simply couldn't afford to keep their companies on pause. We created a poll to find out just how many businesses were grappling with the threat of closure. As we tallied the numbers, we determined that 40% of companies were not going to reopen, a huge and deeply disturbing number.

Just as we were trying to understand how best to address that number, and which policies we could pursue to alleviate the pressure these companies were facing, another tragedy struck. On May 25th, 46-year-old George Floyd was killed in Minneapolis after a white cop knelt on his neck for a sickening 9 minutes and 29 seconds, all while the father of five repeatedly pleaded that he couldn't breathe. As video footage of the incident began to circulate online, people poured into the streets to demand change. How much longer were we all going to watch Black folks die at the hands of police officers and racists, while footage of their hate circulated like wildfire, before something changed?

I could barely watch the video. In George's face, I saw so many other Black men I knew, my sons, brothers, uncles, and even myself, reflected in his dying pleads. It was too much for me to possibly bear. When I spoke with my boys, my voice was softer, tenderness pouring out as I pleaded with them to be careful out there. Even as I said the words, I knew that no matter how careful they were, that wouldn't protect them. It wasn't a lack of care that killed George Floyd, or Philando Castile or Botham Jean or Breonna Taylor or Stephen Clark or Atatiana Jefferson, or any of the dozens of others. It was racism, plain and simple.

While this was happening, protests were raging all over the country, and corporations were beginning to discuss ways to address racism within their own ranks. The U.S. Chamber of Commerce, of which I'm a member, organized a call to deliberate what the group's next steps should be. There were 56 of us on the call, and I was one of the only Black people present. I sat back and listened as the group discussed the idea of a press release, talking through language, and parsing together a few well-meaning but utterly meaningless sentences.

I sat silent for a while, listening and trying to cool the fire I could feel burning at the tip of my tongue. I wanted to give my thoughts, but I knew that to be heard, I had to temper my voice, to soften my outrage, and, instead, make it palatable for the group's ears. Another all too familiar and disgusting symptom of racism was the way we were forced to remain composed in the face of gross injustices just to be heard. But, one thing I knew for sure was, I couldn't get off that call without making my feelings known.

I cleared my throat, and introduced myself. I told the group who I was, and where I was from. Then, I went in.

"The murder of George Floyd, from my perspective, isn't an isolated incident. This isn't about some 'bad apple' cop, or a lack of diversity training. This has everything to do with this country not valuing his life as a Black man. And I say country very intentionally. Across our nation, Black lives are not treated with the same worth and importance as everyone else. These racists can and do shoot us in the streets, on camera, in full view of the public, and get away with it," I said, my voice steady and even. The silence on the other end was so thick and tense, you could cut through it. I continued.

"Now, here we are, one of the largest business federations in the entire world, connected to some of the most profitable and powerful corporations, connected to Congress and the White House. And we're discussing *a press release*? We can do better than that. We *must* do better than that."

My voice cracked slightly as I tried to compose myself and pull back the anger I felt rising in my throat.

"This is an opportunity for us to flex our muscles here. It's our chance to come up with a strategy around education, employment, and to supply diversity and corporate citizenship investment. We have the power, why don't we use it? If we can do that, we can address disparities and inequalities within our nation, and give people an opportunity to present their value to society, to make our country even more competitive, and to actually stand for all of the principles we claim to advocate for. That's what I think we should do."

I exhaled, sat back in my chair, and felt the tension I'd been holding in my shoulders and jaw releasing. For a moment, there was complete silence on the other end; no one said a word. Then, the moderator's low, timid voice crept through the speaker.

"Thanks for that, John. That's something to think about," the voice said dismissively. I gulped loudly, unsure of what to think. The moderator quickly ended the call after that. I sat at my desk, my hands crossed in front of me, and replayed the last few minutes of the call. Had I come on too strong or aggressively? Had I rambled on for too long? I couldn't understand the chilly response. But at the same time, I wasn't prepared to accept their apparent inability to take things further. Did my position in this chamber even matter if I wasn't willing to put my neck out for my people?

I opened my laptop and typed up an email, outlining all of the points I'd made on the call. I addressed it to senior representatives at the U.S. Chamber. After hitting send, I felt a sense of relief. I'd done what I could, and now it was in their hands to determine what came next.

The next day, I got a phone call from Sara Armstrong, President of the U.S. Chamber of Commerce.

"John, I just want you to know that we heard you. We heard every word. And you are absolutely right. We're going to do something about this," Sara said.
 "Wow," I said, barely able to contain my surprise. "I'm so touched, Sara. Really, you've just made my day." I apologized for my rambling during the call. She laughed and reiterated her thanks for my email, and for taking such a strong stance. Then she assured me that some big changes were on the way.

A few weeks later, the U.S. Chamber of Commerce launched the Equality of Opportunity Initiative, a program that would work to close opportunity gaps for Black folks and people of color in six areas: education, employment, entrepreneurship, criminal justice, health, and wealth. They had a massive rollout which was broadcast on CBS, and moderated by Gayle King and Stedman Graham. In addition to the program, the chamber also managed to fundraise more than $100 million from their corporate partners which would be distributed via grants to directly help Black businesses.

Seeing these actions, I really felt the weight of my voice. I'd spoken up and used the platform I had, and real, impactful change was happening. With that win under my belt, AACCNJ began pursuing more vigorous changes. Immediately after, we began hearing complaints from many of our members about how difficult online schooling was for their children, who, due to technology issues and service interruptions, often couldn't get or stay connected. Apparently, the phone and internet companies they had access to in the areas that were all closed due to the imposed state moratorium during the pandemic; a decision that made very little sense to me. Meanwhile, they were open and operating out in the suburbs, which happened to be predominantly white communities.

When I approached Governor Phil Murphy's office with the issue, they were extremely receptive. Within a few days, the necessary policy changes were made to allow technology providers in urban communities to open so they could access technology support to get the kids back online. I felt a sense of pride and confidence that I hadn't felt in a while. I wanted to continue riding that wave, to see what more influence we could have.

At this point, I turned my attention back to the issue of Black businesses and the crisis they were facing staying open. At the direction of the government, banks had been instructed to issue large sums of money to help businesses stay afloat. It was called the Small Business Paycheck Protection Program (PPP). After applying, business owners would receive a loan

Power Moves

to help cover payroll, and other business-related costs. But for some reason, our members were facing so many challenges getting approved. Their applications were repeatedly denied and rejected, and the more I dug, the more sense it made.

Many of the Black business owners who applied for the money were smaller companies. The banks, as it turned out, were getting commissions on the money they distributed to assist companies. This meant that big businesses, those who qualified to receive larger sums of money, were being prioritized over the smaller ones. Once again, our people weren't a priority. AACCNJ fired off a press release relaying our disappointment with the banks, and how they were contributing to an already challenging financial time for Black businesses.

Within a few days, bank CEOs in New Jersey and the New Jersey Banking Association were blowing up my phone. Many of these CEO's asked me to direct member inquiries to them.

"John, believe us man, we're not racist," they all told me. "We want to help." I asked them to put their money where their mouths were. Together, we began discussing a viable strategy. When the second round of PPP loans were ready for distribution, our organization, with the support of the New Jersey Bankers' Association, collected the information of members who needed support. A coalition of nearly 25 banks had come together to help our folks get

236

access to the funds they needed. It was a massive success, and many companies were able to continue their operations, keep their staff employed, and their bills paid.

From there, we were able to take things even further. Leslie Anderson, a brilliant Black woman and President and CEO of the New Jersey Redevelopment Authority (NJRA) partnered with AACCNJ. The goal was to create a program that helped business owners who were suffering extensively to gain access to grants that would cover their rent, while providing them with the support they needed to get their leases extended.

Despite the pandemic's many challenges, it truly brought AACCNJ out of its shell. We recognized an especially dire moment in the lives of many of our members, and we stepped up to the plate to advocate on their behalf. And we were successful in ways that surprised even us. Before COVID-19 wreaked havoc on all of our lives, we'd had plans for the direction we hoped to take our organization in. Those plans, like so many others, were upended. But, in the end, we truly showed up for our members and our community, and forced change on a systemic level. Even for myself, personally, I discovered new depths of inspiration, and a renewed sense of purpose for what was possible for my life.

Chapter 12

The Year of Loss

On a beautiful day in September of 2020, I was making my way through traffic on the New Jersey turnpike, on the way to New York City. The air was warm and my windows were rolled down as the breeze whipped around my face. It was one of those sunny, late afternoons that made you wish summer was endless.

I'd made dinner plans with a friend in the city. We had a habit of never being able to keep our plans, but that day, I'd ended my work day early (something I rarely did) to ensure I made it there. It's strange, but for as many times as I've made that drive from New Jersey to New York City, I never really remember it. That day, however, will remain etched in my memory forever.

When I was nearing the Exit 8 turnpike, my phone started ringing. It was John Jr.

"Hey son," I said, happy to hear from him. "What's going on?"

"Dad," he answered, his voice laced with concern and fear. "Dad, there's something wrong with mom." I shifted slightly in my seat, Lennice's face flashing in my mind.

"Well, what do you mean 'something's wrong with her'? Is she okay?"

"No Dad. I don't know, I just got home and I found her passed out on the dining room floor. I called the ambulance already, they're on the way." John Jr., who was living with his mother at the time, explained that he'd gone to Sam's Club to pick up a few things for Lennice, who was planning a special dinner for her sister and brother-in-law's wedding anniversary. She asked him to call her before he left the store, just in case she needed anything else.

After picking up all of the things on her list, John Jr. called Lennice, but she didn't answer. He called several more times as he paced in line before finally deciding to head home. When he walked into the house, he called out her name, but she didn't answer. He stepped into the kitchen, where he'd last left her, and looked around, but she was nowhere to be found. When he headed towards the dining room, he was stopped dead in his tracks. Lennice was splayed out on the ground, unresponsive.

John Jr. asked me to meet them at the Jefferson Hospital. I immediately took the nearest exit and headed straight toward Langhorne, Pennsylvania, where Lennice lived. I tried not to jump to any conclusions, and to keep my imagination from leading me down a dark path. Instead, I reminisced about our relationship, the first time I saw her, our wedding day, and the life we'd shared together for 30 years. We'd been divorced for 10 years by this point, but it was only in the last few years that we finally found a way to settle into a new dynamic with each other; one less fraught with the wounds of the past. I knew that she'd been deeply hurt when I asked for a divorce, and that she struggled to watch me move on with my life. For years, we barely spoke unless it was absolutely necessary. But by 2018, she began to soften toward me, and the icy walls she built (no doubt to protect herself) slowly collapsed. Regardless of how bitterly things had turned out in our marriage, we were still a family. We had raised three men together, and to do right by them, we had to come together to show them that their family was still intact, even if their parents were no longer a couple.

We began gathering altogether for birthdays and holidays, usually at her house or a restaurant. Food, we realized, was a great olive branch, and an even greater unifier. I loved those dinners, listening to my boys (who are no longer boys at all) share updates on their lives. Lennice and I would sit there in awe of the three brilliant guys we'd created. Whenever she and I were alone, or if the boys were preoccupied with subjects we couldn't keep up with, we reminisced about the old days. We talked about old friends and acquaintances, laughing about past gossip. We'd finally found our groove as friends, and I couldn't fathom the idea of anything bad happening to her.

Around 45 minutes later, I arrived at the hospital. John Jr., two of Lennice's sisters and her brother-in-law, Hosea, were all waiting. I hugged my son, who looked clearly shaken up. We all sat together and Hosea, who's a preacher, led us in prayer.

After an hour, a small convoy of doctors came out and walked over to us. Almost immediately, they started asking questions about Lennice's medical history. We explained that she was a nurse and well-equipped to recognize if something had been wrong with her. She was also asthmatic, but she'd always managed it well.

I held back for a few minutes, just listening. But I could tell by their cryptic line of questioning that her condition was more serious than I'd anticipated. I stayed silent for as long as I could before finally interrupting.

"Can you tell us what's going on? What's wrong with her?" The doctor explained that she'd lost a lot of blood, at which point we all erupted in questions, our concern morphing into panic in a split-second.

"Okay, okay. I need to know who's in charge here?" the head doctor asked, surveying our faces. When they found out I was the ex-husband, I was put in short pants, so to speak, and John Jr. became the point person. He answered their questions as best he could.

Finally, the doctor told us that Lennice would have to be medevaced to a hospital in Philadelphia. My mind turned with questions. The hospital they were taking her to was only around 20 miles away, which was a short enough drive – if she was stable. They told us we could see her briefly.

When I walked into the room, my heart dropped into my stomach. She was laying on the bed, unconscious, surrounded by beeping devices and a concerning number of tubes running into her arms. I looked for bandages, trying to locate the source of her bleeding but I saw nothing. I stared at Lennice, images of her as a beaming, beautiful bride on our wedding day flickered in my mind. She looked so small and helpless, so unlike the woman I'd know for more than 40 years.

At this point, I knew I had to call Joshua and Justin, who were living in California and Florida respectively, to tell them what had happened. I explained that there was a very serious situation with their mom and they needed to get there as soon as possible. I didn't want to alarm them, but I had to emphasize the urgency of the situation. They didn't ask any questions, but said they'd get on a flight immediately.

By the next day, they were both at home and the four of us huddled together to come up with a plan. We went to the new hospital in Philadelphia and were faced with the same question of who was in charge.

Even though Justin was the youngest, we all agreed that he'd take control as the main point of contact.

As we eventually learned, Lennice had suffered a hemorrhagic stroke, which means that a blood vessel in her brain had ruptured. Her condition was severe, and for the next month, we all took shifts spending time in the hospital watching over her. The doctors did brain scans daily, updating us on her condition. They emphasized that if she didn't progress, her deterioration would likely happen quickly. Justin had a close doctor friend he consulted with to help us get a better understanding of what was going on.

Shortly after she was admitted, we learned that Lennice didn't have anything in writing, indicating who'd take control of her affairs. That meant we'd have to go to court to allow Justin to take the reins. Luckily, he also had a lawyer friend who helped walk us through the process.

My childhood friend Kevin Powe, who's now a preacher, came to the hospital every day to pray for a miracle. On one of my shifts, Lennice opened her eyes, something she hadn't done since arriving at the hospital. As her eyes fluttered open, I shot up and grabbed her hand.

"Len, can you see me? Can you see me, Len?" I asked, desperately. It seemed like she was trying to speak, but couldn't. After that, we all felt a surge of hope that she was getting better, holding onto the small threads of progress like a vital life-line. But our hope was short-lived. Her condition deteriorated not long after, and the doctors said that she probably didn't have very much time left.

On November 1, when it had become painfully clear that she was probably going to be leaving us soon, we all went to the hospital to spend her final moments together. We stood over her, clutching her hands, as she took her final breath. As the machine next to her bed buzzed gently, all of the emotions I'd been holding back surged forward.

"How can you leave us, Len? Why now? We're in such a good place. We were doing so well. Remember our last dinner? How hard we all laughed, how happy we were? We're all here. Our boys are all here. How can you do this to us, Len?" The tears flowed uncontrollably, pouring like a deluge down my face. Lennice had been my wife for 30 years. We'd created a beautiful family together. I couldn't fathom living in a world where my boys didn't have their mother, where I didn't have her nurturing presence.

The boys and I clustered together, holding each other and crying, our sorrow coalescing into one massive, devastating buffet of emotions. I never thought when the year began that I'd be saying goodbye to such an important person in my life. I felt unequipped to handle the barrage of sadness flowing through me.

After Lennice's death, we all took turns spending a few final moments with her. We said everything we wished we could've told her, how much we loved and missed her, and how deeply we cherished who she'd been. It was a difficult day, which stretched into difficult weeks after that.

When I left the hospital, I called my friend Kyle Ledford, a funeral director who was also a member of the AACCNJ. He told us to come on by, and my boys and I headed right over. We sat down in his office, and Kyle expressed how sorry he was, extending his condolences.

"Hey, where are the women?" he asked, looking us over. "There are usually women involved in this process, you know?" I raised my eyebrow suspiciously, shaking my head.

"No man, we got this. Me and my guys, we got this. We're doing this." It was true. Lennice's sisters all offered to help out with planning, but my sons and I owed it to her to take the lead. We were her family, her people. We had to do this, to give her a final sendoff worthy of the woman she'd been in our lives.

The guys wrote a fantastic obituary, and set up most of the arrangements on their own. Because Lennice's death happened during the pandemic, we were limited in how many people could attend her funeral. 30, to be exact. It was a minimal number in the endless ocean of folks who loved and cared for her deeply. To ensure anyone who wanted to celebrate her had that opportunity to do so, we live-streamed the whole thing.

The service was absolutely beautiful. It was an open casket, and the boys had worked with their aunts to pick out an outfit Lennice had loved, accessorized with pops of green – her favorite color. She looked simply stunning, and at peace. I said a few words, through a heavy cloud of emotions, my voice threatening to break at any given moment. At the end of the service, the family got the final look. As I stared down into her casket, my heart felt like a cup overflowing with sadness as my sorrow spilled over the edges of my very existence. I thought about the future, and how none of my memories, moving forward, would ever include Lennice again. It was a devastating realization, and left me feeling profoundly lost.

I can confidently say that these were some of the worst days of my life. We lost Lennice so unexpectedly, and so *instantly*. While the period between her hospitalization and her death spanned a little over a month, it felt like it happened within that brief, empty space between an inhale and exhale; a span of time where time didn't exist or even matter.

Though Lennice hadn't been a part of my day-to-day life for a decade, every moment afterwards felt emptier in a way. The world seemed devoid of her presence. If I fixated on it for long enough, I became paralyzed, unable to do or think of anything else. Instead, I threw myself into work, relying on it like a crutch that was becoming more of a third leg. I was used to being laser-focused on work, using it to ignore whatever was emotionally happening to me.

During this time, Justin decided to move back to Trenton to stay with me. Having him around put my soul at ease. I was used to living alone, but being able to see Justin's face every morning before work, and again when I got back home, really helped to keep the sadness at bay, at least to an extent.

John Jr. was still living in Lennice's house, but the three of us – John Jr., Justin and I – hung out every chance we could. Soon after, Josh was forced to return to California after extending his time at home for as long as he possibly could. Even though I didn't exactly address my grief head on, spending time with my sons was healing me in ways I didn't even know. It filled me up to be around them.

I learned something about grief then. It burrowed itself so deeply into your very being until it was indistinguishable from the other parts of you. The grief becomes as normal and mundane as hunger or exhaustion, existing as a mole on the face of your life.

But tragedy, as it turned out, wasn't finished with me just yet. On November 19, I was sitting at my desk in my office, sipping on a cup of hot chocolate, when my cell phone rang. Looking down at the screen, I saw that it was my cousin Harrison, who I hadn't really heard from in some time.

"Hey man, what's going on?" I said, tucking the phone between my ear and shoulder. I leaned back in my chair to relax into the call, but as I listened to Harrison's voice on the other end, I slowly sat up straight, my throat suddenly bone dry.

My brother Eddie, he told me, was dead. He lived in a part of rural Virginia that was sparsely populated, and he'd been found unconscious in his driveway by someone passing by.

"It was his heart and his kidneys, John," Harrison stuttered into the phone. "They just gave out, man." For the first time in a very long time, I felt nothing. I was numb, utterly emotionless, and nearly breathless even. I didn't know what to say or what to do with myself. After Harrison and I hung up, I sat there for Lord knows how long, staring off into the void.

My brother Eddie. My childhood hero. The guy who'd gotten me into cars, who'd taught me how to drive a tractor trailer, to box, to play baseball and basketball, who'd introduced me to new music, gave me fashion advice, and helped to shape the man I eventually became. *Dead*. I pictured his lifeless body sprawled out on the driveway, no one around to notice, no one there to help. I could damn near *touch* the stillness; the silence.

All of a sudden, my emotions were there, present and thick with tension. It felt like a tsunami had just crashed inside me; an ocean of feelings backing up into the tide, leaving the shore of my conscious an emotional desert. But then, there it was, a massive wall of grief and sorrow, surging towards me at a pace and force I couldn't possibly escape.

When I started to think about it, Eddie had been acting strange for a few months. He called me often, and our parents always seemed heavy on his mind. He'd tell me that he'd been dreaming about them more frequently, and he sobbed admitting how much he missed them. He was far more emotionally vulnerable than he'd ever been with me before.

Eddie was a strong guy, he always had been. But when he'd reminisce about the 'good ol' days', and mom and dad, his voice cracked in half. He sounded more like a little boy than my big brother.

"Eddie, man, is everything okay with you?" I'd ask, a little concerned. He was dismissive, saying he was fine. I tried to chalk it up to the realities of an aging mind, and how nostalgia sometimes becomes a frequent companion.

I'd even made the four-hour drive over to Virginia whenever I could, and we'd spend the day together. Eddie would take me to his favorite spot to eat, where the chicken was always hot. We'd sit at a table and laugh and chat for hours before I got in my car and headed back to New Jersey. I never thought the last time I saw him would be the last time I'd ever see him again — a thought that replayed endlessly in my mind.

I couldn't stop wondering if he'd known, if he'd had some inkling that he was going to die soon. When I went to Virginia for Eddie's funeral, I soon got the confirmation I was looking for. I was speaking with my nephews, Eddie's sons, about how he'd been calling more often and the air of melancholy that seemed to surround him. They said he'd been the same with them, something they hadn't quite processed until it was too late. When Eddie's son was going through his father's pickup truck following his death, he'd found paperwork from his doctors indicating that he needed a kidney transplant. Eddie, as it turned out, had never followed up. It was like he'd just given up on life, ready to be reunited with our parents; to fall into a deep and eternal sleep.

At the funeral, I gathered with Eddie's three kids, his two sons and his daughter (who had recently been promoted to Assistant Police Chief in Washington, D.C.) to swap our favorite memories of him. I told the kids that their father had been my hero growing up, and still was. The man I described, they told me, seemed so different from the man he'd aged into, from the father he'd been to them. Life had worn him out and worn him down, that much became clear. But he always remained the well-dressed, popular Eddie from my childhood, who raced cars, and excelled at any sport he tried his hand at.

I wasn't ready to say goodbye to Eddie, just as I hadn't been ready to say goodbye to Lennice. I've learned that in life, there are years that give and there are years that take. For me, 2020 was a year of monumental, life-altering loss, despite how fulfilling and generous it was to me professionally. It made me far more aware of the fragility of life, the transience of it all. At any moment, someone you love dearly can be taken from you. And there isn't a damn thing you can do about it. I won't say it made me more bitter or resentful of life. In fact, I think the opposite is true. I hold my loved ones closer. I express my love more loudly and freely. I'm more grateful than I've ever been, for the people I have and the people I've lost. I try my best to be someone the world will miss when I'm no longer here; to make my impact that will be known and felt by many. Eddie and Lennice both left the world a little better than how they'd found it, in their own ways. They left *me* better than they found me. Even though there's not a day that passes where I don't think of them and miss them dearly, I feel like they live on through me, and through all the people they left behind.

Chapter 13

Moving Forward, Looking Back

We will all, if we're lucky, reach a point in our lives when we begin to look backwards more than forwards; where the past feels more relevant than the future. It isn't because we're nostalgic, or that our best years are behind us (though, they most often are). But because the question of legacy, of our impact and influence, become significantly more urgent.

I find myself there, staring into the looking-glass of my life, more and more often these days. I can't help but wonder how and to whom I'll matter to when I'm no longer physically here. Have I done enough with my time? Have I created a legacy that's sustainable, or one that'll be buried with me? Has my mission to financially empower and uplift Black people, to unleash our potential, been fulfilled? Well, I guess that depends on who you ask.

I remember before I launched AACCNJ, I spoke with Diane Tracy, the woman who'd believed in me so thoroughly back when I was just an ambitious, wide-eyed university graduate. We spoke about my time at the bank, at both Bowery and Chemical, and about how much I'd been able to accomplish in my short time there. At one point, for just a moment, we pondered on how much more I probably could've achieved if I'd just stayed. She admitted that I probably would've become a president, and that I could've made *a lot* of money. And while she was right, that was never my goal in life. I wanted to be someone that made an impact; someone who did meaningful, empowering work.

Instead of abiding by a societally-recognized definition of success, which is usually characterized by the size of your house and bank account, I chose a life of service and contribution.

I'm a servant leader, that's an indisputable fact. Since founding the AACCNJ in 2007, I've lived nearly every day in service to my people. My work isn't, and can't be about solely me. If it was, I would've walked away a long, long time ago in pursuit of greener, less thorny pastures. I could've and would've found a different line of work that paid more money and provided instant results. Reality is, my job is pretty damn difficult.

I've encountered profound wins, sure, but some of my losses have been even more extensive. I've wanted to walk away so many times. To pursue something, anything else, and to leave that seemingly fruitless mission in the past. I've had to wrestle with my own sense of self, and sacrifice my blood, sweat, and tears in pursuit of a dream I wasn't sure could be achieved.

Perhaps even worse than the struggles I've had with myself (or with the purveyors of power who are determined to keep Black folks down) are the ones I've had with my own community, with the very people I was fighting for. The brilliant writer Zora Neale Hurston once said that "all my skinfolk ain't my kinfolk," and I had to learn just how right she was the hardest way possible. Some of the biggest and most persistent obstacles I've faced in seeing my work come to fruition were launched into my path by other Black people.

This is a difficult and uncomfortable conversation to have, and I'm fully aware of that. It's one that feels like it should be conducted in whispered tones or in a locked room somewhere. But I've had to come to terms with this reality, and to face it straight on. It's one of the hardest lessons I've had to learn throughout my entire career.

But it has also helped shape my own approach, and deepened my commitment to Black empowerment, as ironic as that might be. I recall a conversation I had with John Rogers, who is co-CEO of Aerial Investments, the first Black fund management company in the country, and a member of AACCNJ.

"John," he told me, "if you're Black and on a corporate board, you have to be an advocate in the boardroom. You can't be afraid to represent why you're there. That doesn't compromise the integrity of the organization."

As he explained it, whenever we're given access to spaces and places that Black folks haven't necessarily entered before, we have a responsibility to bring others on board with us; to hold the door open behind us. That has been a significant part of the work I've been trying to do. My mission still rests in ensuring that my people get the opportunities that will propel them toward success. Black people have a long history of making this country better, much better, in fact, than it ever could've been without us. Our contributions are invaluable, even if they are rarely acknowledged.

Everything I do, from my work with AACCNJ, to the Trenton chamber, to even my trucking business back in the day, it has always been about uplifting and empowering. Both directly and indirectly, it has always been my life's purpose and passion, though perhaps I didn't always know it. I've tried to instill that as a core value at AACCNJ, especially as we start looking towards a future that may not necessarily have me at the helm. In my tenure as CEO, AACCNJ has accomplished some incredible feats.

In 2016, we helped Mike Ricketts, the founder and president of QPSI, a hugely successful Black business, to secure a $25 million tax credit from the Christie administration. In turn, he used the money to build a 250,000 square-foot packaging services facility. Though he was the first Black person to receive a tax credit that large, he certainly wasn't the last. It was even more impressive considering Ricketts had initially been skeptical of our impact and of what AACCNJ was capable of. He didn't hesitate to become a member and sing our praises after that. In a similar vein, we helped a woman named Adenah Bayoh, who owns six restaurants, receive a 9% tax credit which she used to build affordable housing units.

In fact, AACCNJ has been so impactful in what we've been able to accomplish that we received statewide accreditation with distinction. This was an incredible honor given that only 3% of chambers have received such recognition, despite the 7,000 that currently exist in the U.S. It was announced in a meeting in Florida that I wasn't able to attend, but when I arrived the next day and they shared the news, I instantly burst into tears. I wasn't anticipating having such an emotional reaction, especially in front of a crowd of white folks, but I couldn't contain myself. It felt like all of the hard work – the long days and nights spent cooped up in my office, the difficult conversations, the losses – was finally being recognized. For years, I saw how much the U.S. Chamber of Commerce celebrated the accredited chambers across the country, and how much they valued their contributions. I thought back to all the times I had to explain why we needed a Black Chamber of Commerce in New Jersey, and how frustrating that process had been. I felt validated. Our accreditation demonstrated that our organization was not only best in class, but had been recognized by the largest business federation in the world. Our contributions were changing lives.

In my own personal capacity, I worked with Governor Christie to get a man named Tracy Syphax released from prison. Syphax has since gone on to open his own multi-million dollar businesses, and now mentors and teaches other offenders on entrepreneurship. He's even gotten his record pardoned after 25 years of freedom, and has been living as a productive, tax-paying resident of New Jersey.

Recognition is so fundamental, on both an organizational level and a personal one. Having AACCNJ's value appreciated and rewarded was one of my life's highest points. Another was when, ROI-NJ named me as the #1 most influential person of color in the state for two consecutive years. The award hadn't even been on my radar, and to be perfectly frank, I'd never even considered the possibility of topping such a list. At that time, the lieutenant governor of New Jersey was a Black woman named Sheila Oliver. The attorney general is a person of color, and we even have Senator Cory Booker. My point is, there was no shortage of notable, impressive, and influential people of color in New Jersey. So for me to be named #1, it was proof that I was making a difference. It was evidence that I was on the right track to building a legacy, and not just making moves in my head. I've always thought of myself as an underdog, like I'd had to work twice as hard to get the same respect as some of my peers, especially from my own community. I'm not a preacher or a politician, nor do I carry a title that many people understand or relate to.

When I first started AACCNJ, I began by looking back. I studied those who came before me, and sought to understand and learn from *their* legacies. Booker T. Washington, who established the National Negro Business League. Harry Alford and Kay DeBow Alford, the founders of the National Black Chamber of Commerce, and my treasured mentors and friends. I know that whoever comes after me will also be looking back, and the best I can hope for is that I leave enough behind for them to be inspired by as they use my ending as their beginning.

Aside from the legacy I will leave with AACCNJ, I know that my children are the most important contribution I've made to the world. My sons – John Jr., Joshua and Justin – are living, breathing proof that I came into this world and did, at the very least, one thing right. Given my line of work, they've had to share me with the state of New Jersey and the entire country, for a very long time. But they've never once complained about that. They recognized the importance of my work a long time ago, and honestly it's one of the reasons I've kept going for as long as I have. I'll tell you one thing, it's really hard not to be proud of yourself when you have kids who are as brilliant, thoughtful, kind, and strong as my boys. Regardless of my professional success or all of the things I've been able to accomplish on behalf of Black people in New Jersey, and across the country, I'm most proud to be their dad.

As I continue to trek forward, I often think of something Muhammad Ali once said. "If your dreams don't scare you, they're not big enough." I've never been one to dream small, or even within reason. And I've been in this business long enough to have seen many of my dreams come true. There are a few things I've realized in those moments, throughout the decades of successes and failures, of endless lessons, learning, growing, and evolving. Here are a few:

1. Opportunities exist for everyone, but everyone doesn't exist for the opportunity. There are no shortcuts to success; you have to be committed and dedicated to getting the work done, no matter what. That often means long hours and sleepless nights. But it also means learning how to strike the appropriate balance between resources and relationships, and how to most effectively use both.

2. Acknowledge your shortcomings and ask for help when you need it. There's no shame in not being able to do everything yourself. The only way you can ever be the best at what you do is by bringing your blind spots into clear focus, and actively working on them. If you don't face your problems and limitations head-on while dedicating time to working on them, they'll inevitably reappear, no matter how fast you run away from them. And they'll come back with teeth. So, don't let issues fester.

3. Dream BIG, bigger than what even seems possible. If your 'building of success' only has 10 floors, be prepared to rip the ceiling right off to build an 11th. Pursue the impossible, create long-

term goals that others might scoff at, and then sprint with everything you have towards them.

About the Author

John E. Harmon, Sr. founded the African American Chamber of Commerce of New Jersey (AACCNJ) in 2007, and it is now widely recognized as one of the state's preeminent organizations working towards economic empowerment for Black entrepreneurs and businesses. As the Founder, President and CEO of AACCNJ, Harmon has been a vocal and active advocate on behalf of NJ's 1.2 million African American residents and the over 88,000 Black-owned businesses. Through his work, he's connected countless AACCNJ members and supporters to resources and opportunities that have facilitated their growth and success. Harmon is the former President and CEO of the Metropolitan Trenton African American Chamber of Commerce. In that role, he significantly expanded the group's membership and forged important alliances and partnerships in the public and private sectors.

In his long and tenured career as a chamber executive, Harmon has received numerous awards and honors. In 2024, he was honored with the National Association of Corporate Directors Awards – non-profit governance award. In 2021 and 2022, Harmon was honored by ROI-NJ as the Number 1 Person of Color in NJ. He was recognized as one of the NJ Business Hall of Fame Class of 2021 Laureates. In 2022, NJBIA awarded him the highly coveted title of Executive of the Year. He was also recognized as a

Center of Influence (COI) for the United States Army and was selected as a participant in the Joint Civilian Orientation 2018 Conference hosted by the Secretary of Defense. Harmon was the first individual selected as a member of the host committee for NFL Super Bowl XLVII held in NJ in 2014.

Harmon hosts the award-winning AACCNJ monthly television show "Pathway to Success," as well as the Chamber's weekly radio show "The Empowerment Hour."

Harmon holds an associate degree in Business Administration from Mercer County Community College and holds a Bachelor of Arts degree in Business Management from Fairleigh Dickinson University. In 2022, he was awarded an honorary Doctor of Humane Letters (L.H.D.), honoris causa, from Fairleigh Dickinson University. And in 2024, Harmon was bestowed with an honorary degree of Doctor of Business Administration from Georgian Court University, Lakewood, NJ.

Harmon grew up in a large, working-class family in Trenton, NJ. His father operated his own trucking business; his mother was a factory worker. In high school, Harmon studied auto mechanics and aspired to one day run his own business like his father. He has three sons, John Jr., Joshua, and Justin. He is a member of Higher Ground Interdenominational Church, in Ewing, NJ.